FOOD JAIL

BREAKING THE BARS OF BINGE EATING

STEPHANIE GEORGIOU

WARNING

There are parts of this book that are confronting and graphic and which you may find disturbing. I wanted to keep it as real and honest as possible to give you a true insight into life with an eating disorder. If you are triggered at any point, please seek support. The support section of this book (page 200) lists numbers you can call and resources you can use.

PROLOGUE

She took a long, deep inhale, held it... and released the air out of her mouth as though she'd been holding on to this secret forever. Her heart was beating out of her chest. She was exhausted and depleted. She nervously listened for what could be hiding behind the bathroom door—her parents.

She was hunched over the basin in a cramped bathroom, clinging desperately onto the edges of the sink with her tired arms. Her hands were wet and her knuckles were scabbed and bruised.

Her long, blonde hair—filled with hair extensions because it could never be long enough for her—was tied back. She reluctantly raised her chin to catch her own worst enemy staring back at her in the mirror. Her eyes were bloodshot and tired, with mascara running down her cheeks. 'I am so disgusting,' she thought to herself.

Her cheeks were red and puffy, with inflamed areas due to lack of nutrients. Her stomach ached from all the poking and prodding of her fingers into her belly. She almost didn't recognise the soulless girl staring back at her. 'What have I become?' she whispered under her breath.

This small bathroom was her sanctuary, but also her prison. It was her escape, while it was her addiction. It was the place she always ended up, even after swearing to herself that this would be the last time.

She felt despair to see herself—once a happy girl—doing this over and over again. 'What the fuck is wrong with me?'

Now, she took the fork she'd used and hid it in her pocket.

She didn't brush her teeth. We don't want to ruin that enamel. She knew all the tricks to maintain a perfect white smile that people would always notice.

She regretfully pulled herself back together as best she could and turned the doorknob. The lock popped up and she slowly peered around the corner, sighing in massive relief. No-one was there and the house was pitch-black, as she had left it. Another successful episode without getting caught.

Sometimes she wondered if getting caught would stop her. Was she secretly hoping that someone would find her in this mess and save her? No. That only happened in fairytales.

This was a nightmare that had lasted nine years.

The stairs to her bedroom felt like Mount Everest after an episode. She had nothing left in her... literally. She rolled into bed and shut her eyes, regretting everything. 'How did my life get to this?' she asked herself. She couldn't ask anyone else—it was her secret. She felt guilt, remorse and regret every time after an episode, but these feelings didn't stop her.

Nothing stopped her.

She hoped to wake up and start fresh, like nothing had happened. Sometimes she wished she would never wake up at all.

The first thought she had whenever she woke up was, 'What did I eat last night? That's it, today I'm going to start my diet and eat healthy. It's a new day. No carbs, no junk and no sugar. I can do this.'

I knew this girl. I knew her well.

But her secret, I would never tell.

Every day and every night,

a battle with food she would fight.

All she wanted was to be set free

This girl in Food Jail, this girl, was me.

THANK YOU

First, I want to thank YOU, the reader, for picking up this book: for investing in yourself and for trusting in me. Without your support and belief in me, I would not be here. You are amazing.

To my Instagram family—thank you for your endless support, encouragement and kind words. You're the reason this book made it into your hands. Your support reinforces my passion to educate, motivate and inspire you to know that you can live a better quality of life, whatever that might look like for you.

To my family—where do I even start? How grateful and blessed I am to have you as my family. You continue to support me, unrelentingly, unquestioningly and unconditionally. I haven't always been the best sister, daughter or friend, but you have always loved me for all I am, and for that I am so lucky.

My friends, because you understand me and accept me for who I am. You understand that I may not be present physically and that I like to spend one-on-one time with you and do life a certain way. You accept me and support me and actually know the real me—I love you for that and cannot thank you enough. You make me so happy.

CONTENTS

HOW THIS BOOK WORKS

This book is divided into four parts, to make it simple and user-friendly.

Part One: My Story

Part One gives the raw, dark truth about my past struggles with an eating disorder that went on for nine years. During this time, mental health issues were stigmatised and I felt incredibly ashamed about mine—especially given I was a psychology student. I was reluctant to seek help.

In Part One, I take you to my childhood, teenage years and adolescence, to where it started and how it escalated, and how there were times I didn't see myself living past twenty-one. I wrote poetry about how sad and alone I felt, and this was the only way I expressed my true feelings.

I'm not perfect, but I never strived to be: I just wanted to be happy. I believed happiness would come when I got my dream body. The relentless chase for this ruined me and sent me into a cycle of self-destruction—into Food Jail.

Food Jail is a term I developed to explain what it feels like to be stuck inside a world that revolves around food, body shape and weight. It's a jail that exists within your mind—where, no matter how hard you try to escape, authority figures are waiting to put you back in your cell. You might dream of freedom, but no matter how much you want it, the jailors in your mind keeping bringing you back to prison.

Part Two: Awareness Precedes Change

Part Two of the book explains eating disorders and eating disturbances and how to recognise them. I came up with the term 'eating disturbance' to cover the wide spectrum of eating and body-image difficulties we see (or may not openly see) in today's society. Just because you aren't suffering from an eating disorder, that doesn't mean you don't have some level of challenge towards your approach to food and your body. Every woman I speak to has some sort of battle with their body image.

Part Two covers the diagnosable eating disorders listed in one of the official psychiatric manuals, the *Diagnostic and Statistical Manual of Mental Disorders (DSM)*, as well as the signs and symptoms that you or a loved one might be experiencing. Awareness precedes change: only when you know what you're working with can you put strategies in place to create long-lasting change.

Part Three: Food Freedom in your Mind

My experience led me to crack the binge-eating code and help hundreds of women live more meaningful lives, in my work as a psychologist with profound interest and experience in eating disorders. I escaped from Food Jail, so I can help others going through the same thing with strategies that actually work.

Life isn't about never bingeing again or never having negative thoughts about yourself—it's about creating a life in which bingeing and body image are no longer distressing or at the forefront of your existence. In Part Three of this book, you'll learn the best strategies for managing your mind—your 'cognitions' or thoughts. I train you in how to train yourself to manage everyday situations effectively. A change in your mindset will lead to a reduction in eating-disturbance urges and time spent ruminating on body image, shape and size. You will lead a more fulfilling life.

Part Four: Food Freedom in your Behaviour

The final part of the book aims to address the behavioural elements of an eating disorder or eating disturbance. Habits such as binge-eating, body-checking, mirror-checking and social avoidance are targeted with exposure-therapy techniques. Together, we aim to create a life outside of body shape, size and weight, and prove that you can accept and love yourself the way you are, while still working towards goals that are healthy, realistic and effective.

—————

My clients are amazed by the changes they see in their lives from applying the strategies I teach. I know they work—I've spent more than ten years trying and testing all sorts of techniques. Part Three and Part Four of the book give you an introduction into the world of Food Freedom.

I cannot wait for you to be on this journey with me.

PART ONE
MY STORY

Chapter 1

CHILDHOOD DREAMS

As a child, I was happy. I didn't have a care in the world. No responsibilities or destructive thoughts. No traumatic history or complicated family issues. I truly believe being a child is underrated. Why do we all want to be older?

As a child, I had three dreams—I wanted to be a model, a singer or a dancer. I also wanted to be skinny, beautiful, talented and adored. Who doesn't want that at some point in their life?

I grew up in a Cypriot Greek family with two older sisters whom I've always been close with. My parents are loving, kind and supportive and could not have done a better job at raising three girls. In fact, in hindsight, I was a spoiled brat growing up and got what I wanted all the time! I now realise just how fortunate I was and I feel endless gratitude and work super-hard for what I want.

My parents, however, stopped spoiling me once I was old enough to work in the family business, as most ethnic children did. Once I was four years old, my mother would take us to the Queen Victoria Market every single week, so I naturally felt comfortable around people and started learning the hustle of the market.

My earliest memory of my dream to become a model is of when I was about six years old. I had long, black, straight, silky hair and an adorable smile with my baby teeth. So, my oldest sister dressed me in a funky black-

and-white bandanna, with a black T-shirt and pants, and we had a photo shoot with the aim of sending photos into a modelling agency.

I liked the photos and the way I looked, but there was one photo that bothered me—a lot. Although I had a big grin on my face and I looked happy, I could not draw my attention away from what appeared to be my big belly sticking out. I actually looked pregnant. I wasn't an overweight child: in fact, I was very active and didn't eat many sweets (wow, how that's changed!). Yet, in the photo, I appeared to be pushing my stomach to its maximum, and I had a problem with it. At age six, the demon of body image tainted my mind for the first time.

My mum never wanted me to do modelling; she would say in her heavy Greek accent, 'Models have eating disorders.' However, she wanted to keep me happy and reluctantly sent in a photo to the modelling agency. I bet you can guess which photo she sent in. It was the one in which I had my belly sticking out—I wanted to die of embarrassment and shame in that moment.

I was intensely upset and irate. Models were meant to be skinny, not have giant bellies sticking out! How could my mum have done this to me? I could not get it out of my head. Could she have done it on purpose because she didn't want me to be a model? It was there and then I began to feel inadequate about my stomach. At just six years old, I developed a complex about it, thought it was fat and wanted to be different.

However, I got on with living a normal life. My mum stirred my interests in the way of dancing, gymnastics, piano and more—I was that kid who did every activity under the sun. When I brought up being a model to my mum, she would reiterate her belief that models had eating disorders and I would roll my eyes and believe she just didn't want me to be happy. How wrong could I have been...?

Primary school went by and I entered high school. It felt like such a significant jump, but I was able to make friends and get into the groove. I'd describe myself as an average student academically in Years 7 and 8. Despite having the idea of wanting to be thinner in the back of my mind, I did not take any action until Year 9.

Chapter 2

THE FIRST URGE TO PURGE

When I entered Year 9 at high school, my thoughts about my appearance started to become prominent. I was never overweight, nor did I have low self-esteem: I was active and healthy, just with a strange fixation on my stomach from time to time.

Social media had started to be a 'thing', and I don't know why, but I became obsessed with wanting to be 'shredded' like the body builders I saw. I thought it was normal to want a different body, and that everyone had something they disliked about themselves. I idolised body builders and people with lean muscle, but I didn't know how to look like that. I walked to and from school daily and joined a gym when I was fourteen. As long as I can remember, I've loved exercise and weight training.

When I was fourteen years old, I went to a friend's birthday where we ate a lot of pizza, to the point that I felt sick afterward. I remember this clearly, as the memory was uncomfortable for me for many years.

I remember coming home complaining to my mum about how sick I felt after eating so much. I felt like the pizza and dessert was just sitting in my stomach. Secretly, I also felt guilty that I'd eaten so much junk food, and thought I could never redeem myself. How could I ever achieve a body-builder physique if I was eating pizza? This was the beginning of my first negative, 'all or nothing' thinking pattern about food.

I told my mother that I felt like I wanted to throw up but nothing was coming up. I told her I just needed to get it out of my system to feel better. Mum didn't know about my new food guilt, and she was worried and wanted me to feel better. So, she told me that if I stuck my fingers down my throat, it would make me gag and maybe that could help bring it up— but she added that she didn't want me to do it. I distinctly remember her saying, 'I don't want this to be a habit.' It's almost like she knew, deep down, that this could trigger an eating disorder. Mums have that sixth sense, after all!

I made myself vomit and was glad to rid myself of the disgusting feeling in my stomach. After I brought up the food, I felt a massive relief—physically and emotionally, I felt cleansed. That was the first time it happened.

Who knew that this behaviour would control the next decade of my life?

The photo shoot

My family owns a shop at the Queen Victoria Market in Melbourne, selling fashion jewellery, and I used to work there on weekends. My dad taught me and my two sisters to stand on our own feet as young women and earn our own money.

I was friends with a girl who worked at the market delivering coffee. She was stunning, with a great body, and all I ever wanted was a flat stomach like hers. One week, she came over and told me that she'd been scouted for a modelling agency by a random man on the street wearing a suit. My eyes lit up and my dream of becoming a model reignited. Maybe I could find the man in the suit and become the model I always wanted to be!

I'm a determined person, and I chased down the man in the suit and his modelling agency and scored myself an interview. I arrived for it, so excited and motivated, with my parents. The agency was a shabby office in St Kilda with photos of models on the walls and a messy desk. The man himself was a short, Mauritian buinessman with slicked-back hair in a curly ponytail and very white teeth. His hair was so shiny that I could literally see my reflection in it. He was captivating enough, though, like a car salesman.

He didn't ask me many questions, but explained that I'd need a portfolio of photos to obtain jobs—and he happened to be a photographer who took these photos onsite. He even offered to do my make-up as part of a package, but I declined that. I was so excited. This was it! My dream was finally coming true.

The day of my photo shoot arrived, and I'd spent hundreds of dollars on new clothes for it, as I wanted to bring my A game and make the most of the opportunity. Before I left the house, I ate some lunch while expressing to my mother how excited I was. She came with me, of course, and helped me prepare. She's so supportive and has always told me to go for my dreams.

I didn't know that this shoot was going to be a moment that changed the rest of my life.

At the shoot, there were three styles to be shot, one being a swimsuit look. The bikini I'd brought with me was colourful and bright—kind of like my personality before the shoot! When it was time for the bikini part of the shoot, my greasy agent stood behind the camera and began instructing me on where to position my hands. It seemed relatively normal: 'Put your hands above your head', 'Stick your hips out', 'Twist to the side and put your hand on your hip'. The room felt dark and I was insecure about my body in a bikini, but I believed that I deserved to be there and go for what I wanted, so I tried not to let it show.

Then the agent stopped clicking the camera and slowly moved his head from behind the lens to the side of the camera. He paused. He looked at my body—up and down. He looked disappointed and disgusted. I asked if something was wrong, hugging my arms around my bare body, feeling vulnerable and worried that I wasn't good enough.

Irritably, he asked, 'Did you eat before you came here?'

'Yes, I had two mini bread rolls,' I said, honestly and sheepishly. I felt like I was on trial for eating and was pleading guilty to the crime. Maybe it was a crime in the modelling world!

He rolled his eyes with a frustrated expression. 'You should never eat before a photo shoot—it makes you look bloated.' He was clearly annoyed that I'd wasted his time with my bloated stomach.

I wanted to die at being such an embarrassment and failure. How could I already be sabotaging my dreams? I was fifteen years old and up until that moment I had loved bread. I knew nothing about its nutritional value, but I knew I would give it up to make it as a model.

Below is a picture from this shoot.

Greasy photographer didn't like this swimsuit, either, so I had to go and purchase the bathers he recommended and relive this painful experience at a second shoot. I spent over $80 buying a Cheetah-brand bikini at his request: for a fifteen-year-old, it was expensive! I paid it, though. I wanted nothing more than to succeed.

I later discovered that this man scouted models on a daily basis—he'd even approached the boy who'd later become my first boyfriend, Lucas, and told him that he could be a model. What are the chances? Lucas could see straight through the guy and told me he was a scam artist. He was right. If you google this man's name now, there are many negative reviews. I didn't care; I just wanted to be a model, at any cost. I thought, even if it didn't work out, at least I'd have nice photos. I'm an eternal optimist.

Chapter 3

HIGH-SCHOOL RESTRICTION

In Year 10, I was part of a big, popular group of 'friends', who I soon fell out of friendship with. They were the 'mean girls' of the school and the whole group was corrupt. The moment a girl's back was turned, she was bitched about by the rest of the group. After a boy paid me attention at a party—a boy who another girl in the group liked—I was scorned for being a bad friend. They gave me a hard time and the group's leader wrote me a really mean letter advising me on how to behave.

Now that I look back on it, it was passive aggressive bullying. Luckily, I was smart enough to move away from the group and made a new best friend, named Pam. Pam and I did absolutely everything together: we were inseparable. My parents treated her like their own daughter; they would spoil her, give us lifts everywhere and they even gave her a job at the stall at Queen Victoria Market. It seemed like nothing could ever ruin our friendship—until Pam met a girl named Misty.

Misty seemed like a nice girl, but she came from a very strict family and was barely allowed to go out. I believe it was the strict rules in her household that made her seek thrills elsewhere. Misty shoplifted.

I'd never even thought about shoplifting.

Pam and Misty began shoplifting together: it started with small things such as lip gloss and chocolates from Kmart. Those small accomplishments motivated them to keep going and work together to target more significant items, such as clothing. Soon Pam became addicted, and I was shocked when I went over to her house to find that her room, which had previously been bare, looked like a shop. It was covered in clothes, nail polish and accessories—she was running out of space to put everything she stole! Her parents didn't give her much money, and I found out later that when they asked her where she was getting all these things, she told them that my parents were giving them to her.

My family had opened up their home and their arms for Pam and gave her everything. I never believed she was capable of stealing from them too, but she did. She'd become a kleptomaniac and was out of control. When she worked at the market with us, hundreds of dollars would go missing from the till. We never dreamed she might be the one taking the money.

Then, items around my house started going missing, including a gold belly ring. Pam was incredibly sneaky and secretive and my mother and I began to suspect her, although we didn't want to believe it. Finally, we caught her in the act with hundreds of dollars after a day at work.

I disowned her. There was no closure, no angry speech and no explanation. I accepted it, cut her out and moved on. Everyone at school soon found out what had happened and the mean girls took their attention off me and focused on her. They'd yell out 'Thief!' in the middle of class and follow her around asking why she'd stolen money from me. They bullied her so badly that I told them to stop.

Luckily, Pam was resilient. Could you imagine if she'd taken her life over this mean-girl bullying? How would those girls feel? They're probably reading this right now, as many of them have added me on social media.

I distanced myself from the group and focused on my studies; Pam ended up moving schools. I heard she got fired from a job at a takeaway pizza shop because she was caught stealing from the till. She went downhill; her sole friend wrote all her assignments for her so she wouldn't fail school. This poor girl ended up having a nervous breakdown after Pam stole a wedding ring from her house.

Up until this point, I was bingeing and purging only occasionally—I'd sometimes just eat way too much and get rid of it by making myself vomit. After the drama with Pam, though, my eating disorder increased in intensity, as I felt like I couldn't trust anyone—whereas the eating disorder was always there for me.

New friends, new eating habits

Time passed and I found a new group of friends. It was a small group and we were all very attractive in different ways. I adored how skinny my new friends were and wanted to be the same. I was also trying to 'make it' in the modelling world and after my photo shoot, I really wanted to lose weight.

On top of my intermittent binge-and-purge episodes, I began restricting the amount of food I ate at home, and only took small amounts of food to school. At recess, I'd eat an apple, and at lunch I'd have a low-calorie muesli bar. I'd tear it up into tiny pieces and savour every bite. The canteen became a distant memory. I wondered how my friends could eat hot chips slathered in barbecue sauce and stay the same weight! I was different: I couldn't do that. Models did not eat hot chips and stay skinny.

Then, I stopped eating Mum's food at home and began doing my own grocery-shopping. I stood in the supermarket for hours comparing calories on labels and selecting the foods with the lowest calories, no matter how they tasted. Once I found these 'right foods', they were all I ate day in, day out, because they felt 'safe' and I thought they'd help me achieve my goal of weight loss.

I started keeping a journal of my thoughts, feelings and goals—I still have it today. I was very motivated to lose weight and started weighing myself every day and setting weekly targets. My restriction and eating habits progressively got worse, to the point that I felt paranoid eating in front of people—especially in front of boys. How could a boy ever like me if he knew I ate? The funny thing was, I never had an issue attracting boys! Yet in my head, I never felt skinny enough.

If I got caught in a social situation that involved food, I'd chew gum, say I wasn't hungry and starve myself until I got home. The thing is, I maintained a relatively normal weight, so no-one questioned whether I had an unhealthy relationship with food.

Please remember this: eating disorders come in all shapes and sizes. Yo-yo dieting is where it starts... but not where it ends.

Sweet sixteen

When I was sixteen years old, my dieting became intense. I'd motivate myself to start a new diet plan every week, especially if there was an event coming up. In my journal, I documented forthcoming birthday parties and how much weight I needed to lose in order to feel worthy to attend. I wrote down what I planned to eat and how I planned to lose the weight, surviving on a diet of weight-loss shakes and tuna in springwater. According to my journal, in October 2004 I was consuming three to four diet shakes a day. I recorded my progress in my journal, reporting weight loss, feelings of guilt and also the weird dreams I was having.

My dreams have always been very intense and vivid, and I lucid-dreamed a lot, which is when you know, in a dream, that you're dreaming and can control the dream in any way you want. In my lucid dreams at this time, I'd go into people's houses and eat all their food. It's pretty funny, when you think about it, but also very sad.

However, over time, as my diet restrictions increased, my sadness escalated and my dreams became distressing. I'd dream of gorging on fattening foods and wake up panicked, wondering if you could consume and absorb calories in a dream. When you're trapped in Food Jail, your mind starts thinking the most crazy things!

I was always very active. I walked to and from school every single day, even with a super-heavy schoolbag, exercised in the backyard and played sports. I also loved jazz-dancing and tap-dancing (though I didn't do tap much, as Mum would yell at me for scratching the tiles). I restricted my food intake at school, so when I came home I felt absolutely famished, as though I hadn't eaten for years. I especially craved sugar and felt I needed it to survive. Once I got a first look at and taste of it, I couldn't control myself: my body took over my brain. It tasted like the most incredible thing in the world!

I'd purchase low-fat cake mix with the intention of making a sugar-free cake—but I never got to the baking part. One taste of the cake mix was like cocaine to a drug addict. I was so hungry and deprived that my body behaved like an animal that had been caged up without food. That's exactly what I was doing to my metabolism: caging it and then letting it run wild when it got a taste of freedom.

Coming home from school and eating low-fat cake batter every now and then became a habit. I'd eat wooden spoonful after spoonful, not caring that I got chocolate all around my mouth or on my clothes. I felt high, euphoric and gave zero fucks about anything. The world didn't exist. My eating disorder did not exist. My dissatisfaction with my body didn't exist. Just this moment of pure joy, ecstasy and freedom existed. It was a momentary vacation for my mind after spending every minute of every day thinking about food and my need to lose weight.

What goes up, must come down, however. Shortly after gorging on an entire box of chocolate-cake batter, the euphoria would end and I'd feel sick and guilty, wondering what I'd done and what I'd become. I'd 'given in' and eaten something I chose to label as 'bad'. I'd make myself throw up, then motivate myself to start a new diet plan tomorrow. I'd repeat to myself, 'Tomorrow is a new day, and I'll never eat junk food again.' This is what perpetuated the eating disorder: the belief, every time, that it would be the last time I binged. Little did I know that cake-batter gorging was about to be the least of my problems...

Chapter 4
PILLS WITHOUT THRILLS

My high-school years went on and I got worse. My ways of managing my weight got more extreme and dangerous. I didn't care. I had a goal: to lose weight and live my dream of having the perfect body. I began counting calories and restricting my food even more. I also became obsessed with the idea of taking the diet pills I learned about on dieting websites and forums.

One pill that came up quite a lot was Duromine—a weight-loss drug that should only ever be prescribed to severely obese people. You need a doctor's prescription to obtain it, and a doctor would never prescribe it to someone my size, but I wanted it. I think I was in Year 12 when I got my hands on some.

Duromine's active ingredient is phentermine, which is similar to an amphetamine. It works by stimulating the central nervous system (the nerves and brain), which increases your heart rate and blood pressure and decreases your appetite. It increases your metabolism, keeps you awake, makes your heart beat really fast and suppresses your appetite by controlling the area of your brain involved with hunger. It also has severe side effects—but I didn't care.

The amount of energy Duromine gives you makes you feel superhuman, so you have to take it in the morning to avoid being awake all night.

I didn't. I'd stay up and study until 5 am and I killed my exams. I'd work out at the gym for hours because I just had so much energy. I remember doing two hours on the treadmill and burning around 1800 calories. 'Who needs sleep,' I thought, 'when I'm this productive?'

However, I constantly thought about food and exercise, and especially if I ate something 'bad' (i.e. a forbidden food that was not healthy) I needed to go to the gym. Notice I said 'needed'? It wasn't a choice. The eating-disorder mind compelled me, it became a chore and a demand. I used to drag a friend to a 6 am spin class and I'd exercise with a massive jumper on so I'd sweat more. The thing is, Duromine already causes you to sweat like someone on ecstasy at a rave.

One of the other side effects of Duromine is mood swings. I couldn't understand why I would wake up feeling depressed, why I felt so upset and irritated as I drove into the gym! I'd always been a super-hyper and positive person and depression was quite out of character. At times I felt so low that I didn't want to go on or get out of bed, and I couldn't imagine what the future would look like. I wanted to die young.

I sometimes engaged in self-harm because I didn't know how to express my intense feelings, superficially cutting my wrists to feel better. I wasn't suicidal, I just felt this was the only way I could release and deal with the pain I felt inside. It was also a distraction from all the noise inside my head.

I took a lot of different stimulants over the next few years, including Chinese herbs, but in the end I stopped taking them because of the mood swings. They always made me feel really up and down, yet I felt like they didn't 'work'—nothing was working.

Back in Year 12, I was in a relationship with my first boyfriend, Lucas—the boy the greasy modelling agent had also approached. He'd liked me since Year 10 but I continually rejected him, because I didn't want a boyfriend. I didn't trust many people in general, and I didn't care to be in a relationship or sleep with anyone. I believed that guys just wanted one thing. After years of chasing, though, I realised that this guy was different. He was actually genuine, very attractive and could have any girl he wanted. Why did he want me, a secret bulimic who cut her wrists?

He'd left high school early and became my best friend. He got his driver's licence and would visit me at school and give me lifts home. Lucas had a big heart and my family loved him and were extremely happy when we made it official. I won't forget the day he asked me out. He took me to meet his family at a family gathering, and when his grandmother asked if I was his girlfriend, he turned to me and said, 'Do you want to be my girlfriend?'

When we first got together, I kept my occasional binge-and-purge episodes secret. At times, when we had a fight or I was stressed, I'd binge and purge to make myself feel better. I never actually dealt with my emotions: I just stuffed them with food to avoid feeling, then panicked when I realised I'd gorged 3000 calories. The purging then created a new layer of guilt and pain. After a while, I started writing Lucas a letter after an episode, to explain that I'd made myself vomit. I felt guilty not telling him. Each time, I told him I was over it, and I wanted to believe I was. The secretiveness and lies made me feel like I was cheating on my boyfriend with my eating disorder. But I couldn't stop my addiction—and I wasn't prepared to stop entirely. It was always there for me when he wasn't.

Eventually, he began threatening to tell my family if it ever happened again, so I kept it to myself. I didn't want to upset my family by telling them, when I didn't know how to stop.

As most teenagers do, Lucas would clash with his parents, and one night his mother kicked him out. Being the kind of people they are, my family took him in—Mum said she would never forgive herself if something were to happen to him. He lived in my family home for two years. We had our ups and downs; we were so young.

He was a good person who loved me very much, but like any adolescent male with big muscles and very good looks, he started to show cracks, in the form of small white lies about things he didn't want me to judge him on. Eating disorders and black-and-white thinking go together like bread and butter, and I was no exception: I projected my own desire to be perfect onto others. If my boyfriend slipped up—wasn't perfect—to me it felt like it was over. It was all or nothing. This happened in a few of my relationships over the years: I wanted to kill the relationship before it died so I could move on and not have to deal with it.

At the time, I thought he valued other things, such as his friends, over me, although I now understand. Like everyone, he needed to go out and live his life and I needed to do the same. Even though he wanted to marry me and spend the rest of his life with me, I secretly freaked out that he would be the only man I ever dated. I didn't want to be the reason he woke up in ten years resentful, either, because he hadn't been with another woman and hadn't travelled, and think, 'What the hell have I done with my life?'

I broke up with him once after a mistake he made, but he insisted we get back together. Then in 2010, after four years together, I got very upset about something he'd done and lied about (he did not cheat) and ended it. He never came back and is now married to someone else. I sometimes wonder if things would have turned out differently if I'd stuck by him. Sadly, the black-and-white thinking that led to my eating disorder meant I wouldn't stay in a relationship with someone 'imperfect'.

Chapter 5

WHEN PRODUCTIVITY BECOMES INSANITY

Despite my obsession with food, shape and weight, I set a goal to get over 70 for my Year 12 university entrance score so I would get into psychology. I studied incredibly hard, had after-school tuition and achieved this goal. I was accepted into a Bachelor of Social Science in psychology at Swinburne University. Finally, I'd understand what was wrong with me and learn how to fix myself!

The question was, did I really want to?

I was always a highly motivated individual, obsessed with being productive to feel worthy and good about myself. It got to the point that I felt like nothing I did was good enough. These were self-imposed standards and pressures, by the way: my family supported me in anything I chose to do and were proud of me regardless of my grades and accomplishments.

There were people in my university course who clearly had eating disorders. One girl obviously suffered from anorexia and would take a whole lecture to eat a single banana. I wondered how she could become a psychologist and help people when she needed help herself, yet I also secretly admired her dedication and was subconsciously disappointed that I could not be that disciplined. Of course, here I was with a secret binge-eating and purging disorder—how would I ever become a psychologist and help people?

Even though I was at university, undertaking a bachelor's degree and on my way to achieving my dream of becoming a psychologist, I didn't believe I was doing enough. I helped my parents at the market stall part-time on the weekends, but I felt I could and should be doing more.

Then my sister's friend started a dance studio and needed a receptionist to work weeknights. It was a pole-dance studio for fitness, the first in the industry. 'How exciting!' I thought, 'I've never tried pole-dancing and don't know anything about it.' I went in for a casual interview and was successful at getting the role.

I began working part-time in this new, unique dance studio and saw how successful the business was. I killed it at my role, selling courses and merchandise; the students loved me and so did my boss. We were booked out solid. I took on more shifts, I learned how to instruct, I maximised in any way I could—but that voice didn't leave me… I wanted more. I've always had an entrepreneurial voice and spirit, but when is it constructive and when is it destructive?

My boss opened a second dance-studio location and I became the manager there; again, we were soon absolutely killing it. When my boss opened a third location, I knew that I wanted in on the fourth!

At the age of twenty-two, I decided that I wanted to open up my own business, build it up while I studied, then sell it when I became a psychologist and put my sole focus and energy into that career. It was the ultimate plan. I hadn't studied business and had no business experience, other than in our family business and what I learned through my manager role at the studio. What I did know was that I loved taking risks—'So let's do it,' I thought. 'What's the worst that could happen?'

In between university and working across three of my boss's studios, I was completing planning permits, dealing with insurance, hiring staff, contracting builders and buying stock. In 2010, I opened the business. Every hour of every day was planned and mapped out. It was super-intense, but I did it.

I completed my three-year undergraduate degree in due course, but to become a psychologist you needed to do a minimum of six years' study. I needed to go on to my fourth year, in the form of an honours degree. I applied for honours in every university in the country, spending nights on end at the library filling out applications. I was even prepared to move to

Ballarat (a pretty but cold regional town) to make my dreams come true, for goodness sake.

I was very disappointed that I didn't get into honours the first time I applied, not even in Ballarat! So I worked endlessly on the business and undertook volunteer work to build up my psychological experience and résumé. I also repeated certain subjects at university to get a higher score. Let me say that again: I re-enrolled in a few subjects to get a higher score, while running a business. I had the most amazing teacher and mentor at this time, who believed in me and inspired me in ways no other teacher did. I absolutely killed these subjects and achieved very high marks.

When I started my own pole-dance studio, I started off with myself, a receptionist, two instructors and one pole-dancing room. One year into the business, we were nailing it: we were booked out solid and needed to expand. I built a second pole room and sublet a third room to a beauty therapist: we collaborated and referred clients to one another.

The next year, 2011, I applied again to do an honours degree and I got into Swinburne straight away, no questions asked.

I describe 2011 and 2012 as the years I died. I accomplished so many amazing things and changed many lives through the power of dance and exercise. I was also writing a thesis on body dysmorphic disorder: I was a super-achiever. No-one knew my internal struggle.

Despite undertaking an honours degree, running my own business and continuing to train excessively myself, I still felt I wasn't doing enough. I loved the business and it was my baby, but the drive for perfection was ruining me.

The universities actually require that you not work too much during your honours year, and make you sign a contract stating how many hours you will work. You are told that honours will be the most stressful time in your life, but of course, I believed that was for weak people and I was invincible. However, I did do honours part-time (which felt like full-time) so I could manage the business—not to mention, manage my eating disorder.

Although I appeared to be functioning on the outside, the truth is I didn't know how to deal with stress or my emotions, so after long days and late nights, I turned to food as a stress release and distraction. This propelled my bingeing and purging cycle to the most extreme level it had ever been; I didn't even feel human.

A typical day in my life at this point went like this:

Gym at 6 am and run 4 km.

Go to the dance studio and teach three hours of fitness classes from 8 am to 11 am (believe me, they were strenuous).

Go to university to attend classes, attending to business emails and calls in between (I had the work phone diverted to my mobile so I wouldn't miss a booking). My phone went off constantly and I always had missed calls, emails and messages to attend to. I would pull over while driving to take a credit-card payment. I was relentless in my pursuit to be successful.

After university, go back to the dance studio and teach another three classes, plus private lessons, from 4.30 pm. The last dance class finished at 9.30 pm, so I wouldn't normally get home until 10.30 pm. My mind would be racing and I'd feel pumped up from exercising and not know how to wind down.

I often exercised seven hours per day and I wasn't eating anywhere near enough calories to sustain this level of training. I survived on black coffee, Pre-Workout (a caffeine and guarana supplement drink that suppresses appetite and gives you energy), salad (no dressing) and protein. I avoided carbohydrates, refined sugars and foods that were 'unhealthy'... but it came at a cost. I'd come home severely exhausted and depleted. I felt stressed about how much university work I had to do, the admin work I had to do for the studio, the choreography I had to learn for tomorrow's dance class and all the hats I was trying to wear at once.

I was a positive, influential and encouraging instructor at the business; at university I presented myself as a professional for tutorials, lectures and supervision. To the world I was killing it—and now I look back, I was—but I just did not stop.

I didn't know how to relax or what that looked like. Any time I tried, I felt guilty for not being productive. In order to justify taking time out (to watch a TV show, say), I'd have to be productive during the commercial break. I'd check emails, draft Facebook advert campaigns or do food prep. I was obsessed with not wasting any time and being productive any time that I could. Productivity made me feel significant: if I couldn't have my dream body at that moment, I would dominate in other areas of my life by being productive.

I did have to eat, though, and soon food became my release, my distraction and my escape from my inner world, which was always on the channels labelled 'chaotic' and 'spinning'. During the day, I ate obsessively clean in an attempt to achieve the ultimate physique. However, the minute something 'unhealthy' or 'forbidden' touched my lips, I felt like a failure and would criticise myself for not being able to stick to anything. The belief that I'd failed at eating clean made me eat and eat and eat, and I'd embark on a binge.

The bingeing then sparked massive panic, as I'd consume thousands of calories: although it felt so good in the moment, I was filled with the fear of getting fat. I'd frantically force myself to vomit to release the panic and stress and avoid the potential weight gain. I'd feel cleansed afterward, but only momentarily.

As the months wore on, I binged more frequently and uncontrollably to escape the stress and pressure of everything, then purged to rid myself of it all. In the end, I got to the point that I'd arranged my life to make sure that I could binge and purge nearly every single night. I was spending up to seven hours a day looking at my body in a mirror in short-shorts, and like most fitness instructors, I felt pressure to look a certain way. I was always preoccupied with my stomach, how it looked in the mirror and how it felt. I pinched it every morning as a ritual to measure the fat and not even realise I was doing it. I stared at my stomach in the mirror when I taught fitness classes, and even on days when it did 'look good', I would just say it was the mirrors. I could never win and felt like I was fighting a losing battle.

Until the night I almost lost it all.

Chapter 6

AT THE CROSSROAD

Late one night, after an exhausting day, week and month at work, and after a terrible series of episodes of bingeing and purging, my body and brain gave up. I had burned out completely.

I'd been leaving work at about 10 pm and not focusing. Probably 90 per cent of the time I was in my own head, and I was often unaware of what was going on around me. My family would joke that I never listened to what they said, and it was true. It was as though I lived in the back of my brain and only came out when the world really needed me to. I just did not have the capacity or energy to be present.

That's the thing with an eating disorder: it takes over your soul. You're not even a person anymore. You're just existing, just getting by each day, and you don't care what's going on around you.

That night, I locked up the dance studio, got into my car in the darkness and started to drive home. Stopping at some traffic lights, I noticed the man in the car next to me waving to get my attention. I thought it was a sleazy guy, so I ignored him: I wanted to be left alone by the world. He continued to try to get my attention, however, so I finally made eye contact and I wound my window down. He told me I'd stopped on the wrong side of the road.

Looking forward, I saw four lanes of cars coming towards me. It didn't feel real. I turned just in time onto the correct side of the road.

This incident shook me to my core, and I knew in that moment I couldn't keep living like I was. I couldn't keep living in a world that only existed in my head, not in reality. I decided to stop, and thought I'd be able to— but I couldn't, and I couldn't seem to make myself go get the help I so desperately needed, either.

You already know the basics of what led me to this point, but let me take you inside my head at that time, deep into the brain of a bulimic, so you can understand the disorder better. Let's go on a tour of my Food Jail.

Chapter 7

FROM RESTRICTION TO AFFLICTION

Leading up to the moment I almost drove into four lanes of traffic, as I mentioned, I'd been going through a severe binge-eating and purging phase.

The starting point of the disorder was my over-valuing of body shape, size and weight. I wanted the dream, shredded body, and believed I needed to diet strictly to make this happen. This belief triggered the 'restriction' phase of the eating disorder—during which I cut out processed foods, sugars, carbohydrates and ate a very low-calorie diet.

When I was in the restriction phase, which was 90 per cent of the time, I was a zombie. People would talk to me and I'd blankly stare through them; I wasn't and couldn't be present. Every single morning, I'd go downstairs to the coffee machine in my house looking dead, with black circles around my eyes. Every single day, my mum would ask how I was. She knew that deep down I wasn't happy. It could easily be explained as the result of running a business and completing a university degree at the same time, but it was so much more.

For three years straight, the response I gave Mum was, 'I'm just really tired.' I couldn't even look at her, I was so ashamed about what I'd become. Although my response did not change for three years, Mum still asked me the question every day, looking at me with deep concern.

I covered up just how much I was struggling by never being home. Between my study, running my business and exercising up to seven hours a day, I was hardly there, except for the mornings.

On this quest to achieve my ultimate body through starvation, I weighed my food to the gram and tracked every single thing I ate in MyFitnessPal, a diet-tracking app. I spent hours reading every ingredient on the back of food labels and avoided anything processed. Grocery-shopping was agonising as I would spend hours reading labels to 'pick the right one'. Once I found a food my eating disorder approved of, I stuck to it and did not deviate. I ate the same low-calorie muesli bars, cereal and dairy-free milk for years straight, along with springwater tuna (the tuna you eat when you hate yourself and your life). I weighed myself daily to keep accountable.

I was constantly starving, but this meant that my body was burning fat, right?

After a few days in the restriction phase, I'd have no energy and my mood would begin to rapidly decline. I went from the ultimate motivation to achieve my dream body to desperation, emptiness (literally) and sadness. I would scroll on social media, see all the amazing foods people were eating and think, 'How can they eat that and be happy with themselves?'

My mum cooks the most amazing Greek food, but for YEARS, I politely declined it and she stopped offering, as she knew I was 'on a diet' and wanted to be supportive. I think Mum believed that if she could just help me achieve this goal, I could be happy again. Mum helped me with everything, including food prepping and not having junk food in the house. She respected my goals but could sense my suffering and sadness.

The restriction phase lasted for about one to two weeks, until my body and brain couldn't function anymore. I felt weak, depleted, exhausted (remember, I was exercising up to seven hours per day) and down. I wasn't depressed, but your mood is naturally affected negatively by the physical state of being constantly sleep-deprived and hungry.

I had two brains: 'Eating Disorder Devil Brain' (EDDB) and 'Survival Brain'. The EDDB was clever: it was disguised as a friend that wanted me to achieve my goals. This brain is what kept me in restriction, what kept me strong and kept me going—or so I believed at the time. My survival brain was the brain that was trying to make me eat 'forbidden foods'—but really, it just was trying to keep me alive.

Soon enough, the part of my brain responsible for my hunger (survival brain), which was no longer responding to logic, would start to get my attention and temptation started to creep in. I began to fantasise about all the foods I was craving, imagining eating chocolate doughnuts before I went to sleep at night. Nonetheless, I would wake up and eat my egg-white omelette, tuna and salad for the day. I imagined how amazing life would be if I was allowed to eat bread, but I never thought this could be a possibility. I would fight with the inner voice, telling it that I wouldn't give in and I must stay strong.

Then, as my exhaustion and cognitive function (brain power) continued to decline, I no longer had the power to battle the tempting thoughts. These thoughts were like the devil, but really it was my hunger brain wanting me to survive, trying to speak to my eating disorder (the real devil!) in a language it could understand. My survival brain would say, 'Come on, you've been so good all week: one biscuit won't hurt.' A biscuit right now does sound like heaven on earth, I would think.

I'd start to move from complete rejection of these thoughts to justification and rationalisation. I'd think about how I was going to the gym later and would 'burn it off'. My hungry, deprived brain was trying in any way it could to justify getting out of Food Jail. It was desperate to have its need met—survival.

Most of my time at this point was spent obsessing about foods I was depriving myself of—foods I would never touch while I was in the Food Jail, restriction phase. I couldn't concentrate or focus on anything else; all my energy was spent on the battle between my two brains.

The mental battle of the brains soon hit its peak and I just wanted the noise to end, so I would 'give in' and eat the biscuit I'd been craving. The first bite tasted so incredible and liberating, like I'd just hit the jackpot of life. It was only one bite of a biscuit—although it tasted like the tears of God during restriction—but it set off alarm bells and my EDDB awoke again.

The EDDB saw me take a bite of that biscuit and immediately said, 'What have you done? You can't stick to anything! You've failed, so you might as well eat the rest of the biscuit.' Starting to panic, I'd eat quickly to try to block out the voice of the EDDB. I believed that I'd 'stuffed up', so I'd eat two biscuits, three and then four. My panic increased, as did my eating speed and urgency to eat all the biscuits. Out of sight is out of mind, right?

If only it stopped there... This is the beginning of the binge phase.

Chapter 8

THE BINGE THAT MAKES YOU CRINGE

In the minute after my Eating Disorder Devil Brain (EDDB) reasserted itself, I would have downed a box of Oreos like it was nothing. The stress of that made me want to keep eating, for two reasons. One reason was to distract myself from the mistake I made by breaking my diet and the negative feelings associated with that; the other reason was that, since I had 'ruined my diet', I might as well keep going. My survival brain was so starved that it then took control, and my logical brain didn't stand a chance.

My logical brain—my reasoning and judgement—was shut down by the survival brain when I entered binge mode, so my survival brain could do what it needed to do to ensure I didn't die of starvation. You might know the survival brain as the part of the brain that gets activated when you are stressed or sense danger—the 'fight or flight' part.

In this triggered, fight or flight state, I was like a hungry tiger, careless of myself and everyone around me. My survival brain was desperate for me to eat, since it didn't know when or for how long I would restrict it again.

In my binge trance, nothing mattered. I would kill just to be left alone with my binge. I would have broken up with my boyfriend just to get him out of the house so I could binge (although I never needed to do this). I would lie through my teeth to get my fix. The binge trance was a drug, an addiction; it was a part of my life that I just accepted would be there forever. I worked around its demands.

I spent copious amounts of money experiencing 'dream foods' that I would never normally touch and that I had spent years depriving myself of—pastries, fast food, chocolate and ice cream, just to name a few favourites. The binge trance turned me into a kid in a candy store with no rules or restrictions. For a short time, I was set free from the angry, judgey food monster breathing down my neck telling me 'NO'.

When I went out to buy food, I felt judged and scrutinised by the people in the store, as if I were wearing a 'Binge-eating bulimic' sign on my forehead. I could feel everyone's eyes on me, like they knew what I was really going to do with that family-sized pizza, litre of ice cream and block of chocolate.

I didn't wait until I got home to start the binge—I couldn't. I knew how quickly this would be over, so I needed to start immediately to make the most of it. I'd buy 'pre-binge food' to eat on the car ride home to the 'ultimate binge'. Nothing like some binge-appetisers to get the party started! Drive-through takeaway was a godsend, because of the increased anonymity and confidentiality. I could get a McDonald's Oreo McFlurry with extra sundae sauce and no-one would judge me. If someone I knew did see me, though, I had a story planned.

I was terrified of running into someone who would see what I actually ate while I was out there pretending to be healthy, gluten-free or vegan (whichever front we chose that week). Which image you try to portray to the world doesn't matter: when you're a binger, you feel like a fraud constantly.

The binge-eating trance is like lucid dreaming. Remember my lucid dreaming as a teenager, when I knew I was dreaming and could control the dream in any way I wanted? Being in a binge trance is like that, but it's real. I got to live in a fantasy and eat anything I wanted to and not care. This is what drove my bingeing behaviour: the illusion of fantasy, escape and perceived satisfaction.

The typical binge

Warning: what follows is graphic and could be triggering.

A typical binge would start with something solid and substantial like bread, pasta, pizza or rice covered in fatty toppings. During a typical binge,

I would easily consume six slices of bread with melted cheese, peanut butter or chocolate. I'd cover the bread in butter, something I would never normally eat—binge foods were 'forbidden foods' that would make you 'fat'.

After I ate the bread, I would go on to something that had liquid in it, to soften the bread. If you don't consume enough liquid during a binge, it's very painful to then purge. Imagine bringing dry, golf-ball-sized pieces of bread up your throat, which is probably already sensitive. However, you don't want to waste your liquid calories and stomach space on water! Us bulimics are just as calorie-effective in a binge trance, but in the opposite way. I'd drink full-cream milk, full-fat ice cream, milkshakes and hot chocolate. I felt sick and disgusted, but not even Jesus himself could drag me away from a binge. It is almost a thrill to try all these forbidden foods, which you believe won't affect your body because you're going to vomit them back up. How wrong this theory is for most bulimics, you will learn later.

After that, I moved on to cereal—a binge-eater's favourite! Is there anything better than eating cereal at night? There's something so comforting about it. Maybe it takes us back to our childhood, when it was okay to eat cereal and we didn't feel guilty about eating carbs late at night that we weren't going to burn off. I'd eat not one, not two, but FOUR bowls of cereal, topped with anything that could be a potential topping. You name it, I would coat my bowls of cereal in it: peanut butter, ice cream, biscuits, chocolate, honey, maple syrup, Nutella. Then I'd heat it up in the microwave, because warm food was comforting to me. I would even eat in front of the microwave while I wait for the binge food to heat. It didn't matter what I ate. In my head, it was just coming straight back out.

After a binge, sometimes I couldn't physically walk to the bathroom because my stomach protruded from being so full and this caused physical pain. I was legitimately pregnant with a binge baby. So I'd lie down in front of the fire like a beached, depressed whale, so tired and exhausted, wondering how my life had come to this. At times, I wished I could just disappear to avoid having to deal with this life that was controlling me.

During a binge-eating trance, though, my mind never considered the pain or regret I'd feel afterward. Your brain is in survival mode and your frontal lobe—your logical reasoning, perception and judgement—is closed for the time being. Going on a binge is like the best mental vacation you can go on; but it's short-lived and has a deep, dark comedown.

Chapter 9

THE PURGE FOLLOWING THE SPLURGE

Following the binge high comes the sudden realisation that I feel sick, full and exhausted, and I know I need to take myself to the bathroom and get rid of all the sinful foods I've consumed. I was always torn between not wanting to do this and wanting to delay it by bingeing even more, but every minute you waste agonising over this, calories are being absorbed. It's a ticking time bomb, so I would hype myself up to do it. I'd tell myself it would only take two minutes, and I would feel so much better afterwards. Us bulimics are the most motivated and determined people you will meet.

So I reluctantly but desperately made my way to the bathroom or toilet, full of dread. I dreaded someone walking in and discovering my secret—and ruining my progress. I dreaded giving myself stomach ulcers. I dreaded my beautiful white teeth rotting because my enamel had worn off due to the acid in my vomit, and I dreaded bursting capillaries in my face.

Purging isn't pretty, but I promised you'd get the raw truth, so please don't judge me. When I purged, I would use one hand to press against my stomach and stick the other down my throat. I usually used my fingers to instigate the gag reflex, but at times I used the plastic handle of a fork or the back of a toothbrush. Plastic was more painful, but was sometimes more efficient and effective for stubborn foods. It also gave your fingers a break if you were beginning to get marks on the knuckles from the stomach acid.

The first gag was always the hardest to initiate, as it was usually liquid or stomach acid and this could sometimes cause you to panic—you worry the food has already dissolved into your system (i.e. straight to your fat cells). However, once you got some momentum, the vomit would get increasingly thick and consistent. Seeing thick chocolate, chunks of bread or streams of ice cream created a false sense of reassurance and relief. You felt like a disgrace to humanity for doing this, but you also felt safe from becoming fat.

You would hurry to wash it down the sink, constantly listening out for the noise of someone coming home. It's so stressful. I know girls who actually moved out of home to keep their eating disorder a secret from family and friends. This is what I mean about living a life around the eating disorder. It controls your universe and you revolve your life around it.

During the purge, your nose and eyes become runny, your throat hurts and you feel like an unattractive, desperate piece of shit that doesn't deserve to be here, throwing up beautiful, expensive food while someone is dying in Africa of starvation. The guilt and emotional turmoil is torture, but you can't stop.

Sometimes there may be barriers or situations you're not prepared for: for example, small sink holes, drains blocking up and overflowing puke. However, nothing will stop a bulimic on a mission to accomplish their goal. Although I hardly purged in public, I'd still resort to pretty desperate measures to make the food go away, so I could try to forget about how low I'd sunk.

A purge can last anywhere between five to twenty minutes—or it can last hours, depending on how quickly you can get the food out and how satisfied you are with the output.

The double binge

Sometimes I'd feel compelled against my will to double binge. This meant bingeing and purging again after the initial purge! I'd be exhausted emotionally and physically, but the jailor in my head would tell me to binge and purge again to make the most of it. It was like self-induced gastro or food poisoning. Why was I doing this to myself? Did I hate myself that much?

I'd go to bed feeling horrible about my behaviour and guilty about all the 'bad food' I'd consumed, telling myself this would be the last time. This thought is comforting, but never true. I'd promise myself that tomorrow would be healthier and I'd eat clean to get back on track. I'd plan a new eating regimen, hopeful that this might stop me from becoming a bulimic monster again.

The morning after

Following a binge and purge, you return to the restriction phase. I would wake up the next day and relish those couple of moments in the morning before I remembered what I'd done the night before. Once I did, the feelings of guilt and failure came back and I just wanted something to erase my memory.

Physically, my stomach would be bloated and hurting and my digestion impaired. Bulimics who take laxatives to get the last bit out would be running to the toilet at this point. They'd cancel work and any appointments, as they wouldn't be able to get off the toilet and would feel so emotionally low about the night before. It's like a hangover: you can't face the world. Not like this. This isn't who you are to the world.

I'd self-soothe by telling myself again that today was a new day and I would only eat clean foods. The bleak hope that I could get back on track was the only thing that got me out of bed. Well, that and my desire to not disappoint others who believed I was something. I motivated myself to start a new diet plan and to avoid any social situations that might derail it.

The restriction phase isolates you from friends, relationships and your family. Your eating disturbance is your best friend: it will always be there for you and will never tell anyone your secret. You stop fighting it, because it's too exhausting.

This is Food Jail. The cycle of restriction, bingeing and purging becomes your world.

Every time, you tell yourself that it's only going to happen this once—that when you wake up in the morning, everything will be different. Every time, your brain convinces you to have just one bite to satisfy the itch, but the guilt of breaking a dietary rule means that it's never one bite. It's all or nothing. You lie to yourself over and over to get your logical brain to shut up, so you can give in to the desire to binge and to relax about your problems for the duration of that binge. Your brain knows it's a trick, but you still do it.

I used to be so exhausted after a binge and purge episode that I'd sleep for fourteen hours straight. As well as the bloating and stomach pain, my throat would hurt from sticking my fingers or the back of a fork down it, and sometimes the top of my knuckles would be bruised and scabbed. Your stomach and digestive system take a big hit too, of course. Ten years later, I believe I still have inflammatory damage from the torture I put my stomach through.

My skin would break out from lack of vitamins and my capillaries would burst, causing my skin to go red. During my adolescence I also developed acne. It was the most debilitating experience—acne is a significant factor in the depression of Australian teenagers.

I isolated myself socially, rejecting my friends' calls and skipping social events because I just wanted to be alone. I missed birthday parties, going-away events—even for my close family. I didn't care. Everyone knew that I was super-busy running my business and completing my honours and then my master's degree, so they understood. I had the perfect excuse to not partake in social events, but it kept my problem alive.

When this vicious bingeing and purging cycle becomes normal for you, it's like being in a dark hole that you can't see out of. You can only see what's in front of you: bingeing and purging and your next fix.

I needed help badly, but even after the traffic-light incident, I couldn't seem to make myself stop and go get that help.

Chapter 10

THE STRAW THAT BROKE THE BULIMIC'S BACK

At Easter 2011, I hit the lowest point in my life. I'd thought, after the traffic-light incident, I'd be able to stop bingeing and purging, but I hadn't even been able to make myself go seek help.

Events such as Easter, Christmas and birthdays, which should be joyful and exciting, were extremely stressful, challenging, triggering and exhausting for me. I felt intense guilt about how lucky I was to have an amazing family who celebrated these events with so much love and effort, yet all I could think about was how I could avoid bingeing.

Year after year, I deprived myself of Easter eggs and hot cross buns and watched others enjoy them. I believed that I was different, that I could never have these foods if I was to achieve my dream physique and be a winner. I wondered how people could eat them like it was nothing and not think twice about it. I longed to feel 'normal and part of the tradition' but I felt I didn't deserve to have any treats—not until I had the 'dream body' I'd been trying to reach for years on end.

I just wanted to be normal and have an Easter egg—so I would. Soon after, the remorseful thoughts started flooding through my head. 'I should have known better, I've ruined everything, I can never stick to anything and I will never lose weight.' I concluded that I was a failure and would never be good enough. I'd start to panic. I felt as though I'd committed a crime and ruined everything.

The initial restriction (not allowing myself to have Easter eggs) followed by breaking a dietary rule (having an Easter egg) would trigger a massive binge in which I consumed any Easter egg or food item in sight. I was unstoppable. You can't think straight when you're in a binge trance.

In 2011, my Easter-egg bingeing frenzy occurred when my family went to Greek church. We had many Easter traditions as a family. I used to go to church as well, when I believed in something and didn't feel like such a guilty criminal with my secret addiction. But I'd stopped seeing this time of year as about Easter or church: all the Eating Disorder Devil Brain (EDDB) saw was a window of opportunity to binge. The emaciated tiger had been left at home alone, and was about to be let out of its cage into a room full of food.

I launched, and I launched hard. I ate everything and anything in sight. Easter eggs, Easter eggs and more. I just wanted to feel good, satisfied and satiated. I wasn't even aware of what I was eating; all I knew was that I had a deadline and needed to be quick and efficient. I accomplished my goal and returned to my seat like nothing had happened. My exterior was nonchalant, polished and unsuspicious, but inside I was like a burns victim, with all my emotional turmoil and guilt eating away at my flesh.

I have two older sisters, Georgia and Chloe. Georgia, the eldest, has two boys; Chloe is the middle child and is always so generous and the best auntie to Georgia's children. When Chloe returned from church with my parents, she was absolutely devastated and irate to find I had eaten all the chocolate presents she'd got for the kids. Whoops...

She cursed and yelled at me, incredibly angry. Every year, she put so much effort into my nephews, whereas I couldn't even remember when their birthdays were without a reminder. I'd labelled myself the bad auntie and there I stayed.

I defended myself quietly by saying I didn't know that the Easter eggs were a gift for them. There is nothing you can do when you have an eating disorder but bear the wrath of the people you disappoint and wait for it to be over. Deep down, they know you're struggling, but are frustrated because they don't know how to help you. Your denial infuriates them. Denying you have a problem, denying you know where the whole packet of Tim Tams went, denying the wrappers that they find everywhere. You can't have a logical conversation, because a) your brain isn't functioning and b) they will never understand your problem.

I felt incredibly guilty and awful, but I had no energy to fight—she had every right to be angry.

Then Mum broke down and yelled and yelled at me in a way that showed she had been holding on to this for many years. 'You have an eating disorder! Admit it!' She cursed at me and urged me to admit I had an eating disorder and needed help.

I couldn't handle it. I ran out of the house. I left my family at Easter and I ran and I ran and I ran.

I ran until I couldn't breathe and until my legs couldn't run any further. I cried and I cried, feeling so trapped and so far away from my family, which was perfect but didn't understand my pain. I continued to walk and walk, for five hours straight, across Melbourne to my dance studio. I felt so alone. No-one knew what I was going through and I believed all they would do was judge me. This wasn't true, but it was how I felt.

I'd distanced from my family, my friends and anyone who ever tried to get close to me. What did they know? They couldn't help me: I couldn't even help myself. How was I ever going to be a psychologist and help other people when I was in such a state? I'd hit a point of utter despair.

When I reached my dance studio, I immersed myself in work, because productivity gave me some sense of self-worth. A friend started an online chat and I told her about my massive walk. She offered to come pick me up and take me home.

Chapter 11

IT'S NOW OR NEVER

The next morning, I woke with a heavy heart. I'd destroyed our family Easter, run away from home and caused a breakdown.

I knew I wasn't happy and couldn't go on living life around my eating disorder and acting like it was not a big deal. It was a big deal. It was impacting my day-to-day functioning: which is a criteria for diagnosis of a psychological disorder—it needs to impair your normal, day-to-day functioning. I was constantly tired and not present, my cognitive function and memory had been affected and I'd nearly killed myself not realising I was driving on the wrong side of the road. I woke up and realised that I couldn't keep going like this. I wasn't living, I was existing. I was participating in this amazing life and not enjoying it.

What would life look like for me if I didn't change it or get help? Why had I accepted this as my life for years? What was I gaining from it?

I knew it in my heart: it was now or never. I couldn't manage it on my own. If I could, I would have by now. Mental illness was not as accepted back then, so I was hesitant to open up to anyone. Especially because I was studying to be a psychologist: I believed I should have my shit together.

I ordered some self-help books. I didn't use them. It's embarrassing carrying around a book that says 'OVERCOMING BULIMIA' on the front cover! I needed more help than this. So I told myself that no-one had to know I was getting help, and that I would privately see a doctor far away from where I lived so that no-one would see me or find out. I googled how to get a mental health treatment plan and reluctantly dragged myself to the doctor.

At the doctor's office, I remember feeling so embarrassed that I couldn't talk about the issue or bring it up. I couldn't even tell the doctor I had an eating disorder. However, I got a referral to see a psychologist for ten sessions on a free mental health care plan, and was proud that I had made it that far.

I arrived at my first appointment with the psychologist not knowing what to expect. It was a little old house. I parked my car out the front and pressed the buzzer on the gate. 'Come in,' an old male voice said on the intercom. It was creepy, I'm not going to lie. 'Am I going to die?' I thought.

I sat in a waiting room with furniture and magazines that looked like they were from 1982. I felt weird. The lady before me came out of the psychologist's office, crying. (I later called her the weeping widow, as she came out crying after every appointment.) Then a tall, older man with curly grey hair welcomed me into his office. 'How is this guy going to help me?' I thought.

He didn't talk much, just kind of looked at me while I manically talked away to fill the awkward silence. Even with my psychological training, I couldn't pick what approach he was using.

I was sceptical about this psychologist's vibe, so I thought I'd challenge him in my first session. I'll never forget what he said to me when I did just that.

'So... have you ever seen a psychologist?' I asked curiously.

He smiled and calmly replied, 'I couldn't imagine anyone doing this type of work without once having seen a psychologist. I was a patient for years.'

This guy was now the Dalai Lama to me. I share this same piece of wisdom with my clients when they ask this question.

I continued therapy weekly to fortnightly for the ten sessions and followed his instructions. I recall always being quite manic, fast-paced and constantly on the go. I even talked rapidly, as though I didn't have time to talk about my problems. I just wanted solutions. I'd wear my blue gym shorts, leggings or trackies and wonder if he thought I was fat or if I looked fat.

I'd come to appointments straight from work, and it was the only hour of my week when I wasn't a slave to my phone and emails. My phone would be on silent; after a session I would have fifteen missed calls from the business—and this was usually on a Friday afternoon! But it was the one hour of the week which was mine. It felt like heaven.

I expected some rigorous cognitive behavioural therapy program when I entered therapy, but all my psychologist did was get to know me. When I told him about my bulimia, but he didn't say a thing, just stayed calm and chilled. There continued to be awkward silences that I felt I needed to fill. I remember thinking, 'Umm, hello? Where does the program come in? How is this going to help me?'

He told me to spend more time with my family and to keep a journal. He said specifically, 'Don't worry about writing a book, just write for you.' It's almost like he knew that my desire to achieve and be productive meant that I would feel like I should be writing a book in order to justify writing for myself. He also encouraged me to write down my dreams and bring them in. He would analyse them and he was incredibly accurate. As I've mentioned, I had the most intense and strange dreams of my life when I had an eating disorder. This psychologist felt very Freudian to me. (A Freudian is a therapist who subscribes to the techniques for treating patients that well-known psychoanalyst Sigmund Freud developed in the late 1800s. A Freudian analyst typically spends a lot of time exploring their patient's childhood, interpreting dreams and encouraging free association, which is talking freely about whatever comes into the patient's head.)

On the psychologist's recommendation, I began taking half a day off on Thursdays, and called this 'secret Thursdays'. I'd use the time to go out for dinner with a friend, but I didn't tell anyone about it. I didn't want anyone to know I wasn't working and I didn't want people to bombard me in my only time off.

It was a start, but I definitely wasn't 'fixed'. Below is an extract from a journal entry I wrote during this period. I was twenty-three years old.

November 1st, 2011

The feeling of guilt and shame stops me writing. I've wanted to write a long time now. I visited my psychologist last Friday, October 21st. This was a glorious week, being the first week I could walk in and say I hadn't binged for one week. I still allowed myself food at night, but I went easy on myself, as it was my week off after uni and I didn't want to launch into a rigorous diet for fear of failure.

However, Saturday evening we went out. Prior to this I went shopping with a friend. It had been so long since I had been shopping, as I hate it for a number of reasons. Firstly, I hate going shopping if I consciously know I haven't lost weight. As stupid as it sounds, I don't feel I deserve clothes unless my body looks good. After trying on numerous dresses, which I felt grotesque and large in, I wanted to cry and give up. Everyone was going to be at this event on Saturday. I had no outfit and felt depressed and all I wanted to do was go to the gym or cry. I finally found a dress I thought was okay, except my stomach looked fat in it. I planned to wear my hair extensions straight and hold my clutch in front of my tummy so no-one would see it. I also planned that if I were to drink, I would only have shots to minimise bloating of the stomach. Although this seems excessive, it's how I legitimately felt all night long. I felt too fat to be wearing [a dress] this colour. [It was orange.]

I spent the night with my male friends. While others reported countless men looking at me, I felt that no-one was approaching me. I woke up the next day feeling disheartened. I hadn't met a new man or at least interacted with one who wasn't a good friend of mine. I instantly started to think it was the dress and I started to regret wearing it. Having these negative thoughts and concluding that I did not attract men because of my size, I got nervous and, after eating a healthy breakfast on Sunday, started stuffing my face with food. Guys didn't want me for my weight, so what's the point? I thought. Why not binge on more food for about two minutes of satisfaction and distraction from my thoughts. I might as well get rid of whatever's inside me and maybe I can feel better about myself.

What made the situation even worse was that we had a friend of ours over and we had to be at a baby's first birthday party. I didn't care, all I wanted to do was binge, purge and feel as empty on the inside as I felt on the outside. It was horrible. When I got to the party, I was surprised and saddened when people informed me that my voice sounded husky. It wasn't like I was going to say, yeh I spent the last moments getting ready at home by sticking the end of a spoon down my throat to get rid of the sins I'd consumed.

This journal entry basically describes my mid-twenties. My world revolved around the eating disorder; my every move, decision, event and activity was dictated by it. The eating disorder was the sun, and it only went away when I was sleeping, except for when it found me in my nightmares.

After my ten sessions with the psychologist finished, I went overseas on holidays with friends for five weeks, and I had no episodes at all while I was away. When I got back, though, the stress of the business and study had me straight back in my old habits. In 2014 and 2015, I finished the final two years of my psychology qualification—a master's degree—while running my pole-dancing business, and the eating disorder was always there when I needed comfort.

I decided if things were to change for good, I would need to flip the situation and create a life outside the eating disorder, not around it. I needed a life where it didn't fit in, it couldn't fit in and if it reared its ugly head, I'd be prepared. I'd acknowledge it for what it was—an ugly head trying to derail me from my attempts to live a full life.

I became obsessed with learning about eating disorders. I read every self-help book under the sun, listened to the best audiobooks, watched YouTube and even listened to the anecdotal stories of others. As I still yearned for answers as to why I wasn't 'fixed' yet, I saw other psychologists, psychotherapists and I even had hypnosis because I thought I had an addiction to chocolate!

I gained a lot of knowledge—but it didn't fix my problem or stop my bingeing.

In 2015, however, once I qualified as a psychologist, I sold my five-year-old business as I'd planned to focus on my new career. And slowly I began getting better.

Today, when people ask me how I overcame bulimia, I can't give credit to a single psychologist or therapy technique. It was all me and continues to be all me, every hour of every day. Through my past, my own clients and more than ten years of clinical experience and studying the topic, I learned one thing that they don't teach you in self-help books and courses. I've applied this secret to my treatment with clients—and it works. I even teach this to friends and family members who don't have eating disorders but want to change ineffective eating habits.

I used everything I learned, but that's not what helped me overcome my own demons. You see, the answer, the strategy and the solution is not just external.

It wasn't, 'What did I need to do?' to be fixed, it was 'Who did I need to become?' in order to not have an eating disorder.

The answer to overcoming your demons is internal. It's inside of you. It is you—every second, every hour of every day—that makes a decision to either move in the direction of the eating disorder or move away from it, and to become a person who doesn't have that disorder.

The knowledge and techniques you acquire in therapy are great, but not enough. It might feel wrong and uncomfortable at the time—but it's you that either feeds your eating disturbance or moves you towards normality and freedom. The reason it's so hard and that so many people relapse is because what is right and what is recovery feels wrong when you're living in the world of an eating disorder.

I've learned all the tricks of Food Jail. I know why it feels right when it's really wrong. I know why the behaviours feel good and moments later feel like the biggest regret of your life. I've spent years deciphering the eating-disorder code and I'm here to share with you how you can break the bars and escape Food Jail.

If you're living in another type of jail, whether it be Alcohol Jail, Drug Jail or Anger Jail, read on. My strategies are universal and can be applied to any type of jail. I'll teach you how to break the bars and be free, physically, socially and psychologically.

PART TWO

AWARENESS PRECEDES CHANGE

In order to make changes in your life, you first need to become aware of the concern or problem. You cannot change what you don't acknowledge. Awareness precedes change.

This is why you see people who have the same behaviour, the same habits and the same attitude of 'Nothing ever changes' year after year. This is why they always get the same results, or should I say lack of results. They haven't been 100 per cent raw, honest and vulnerable with themselves. I get it, don't worry. I know how uncomfortable it feels to admit you have a problem or addiction, or that something isn't quite right. We all have something going on and ignorance is sometimes bliss in the short term.

I've had to admit this to myself, even as a psychologist, with areas of my life I want to improve on, and there's nothing wrong with that! If acknowledging my problem is going to help me long term, then why wouldn't I choose to experience the short-term discomfort? If moving on forever means I have to get real with myself—I need to try, and really try.

Now it's your turn, and I'm here for you.

In this part of the book, together, we confront your demons head on with no regrets, no judgements and, most important of all—no denial. I need you to be the most open, honest and vulnerable you have ever been. I need you to step away from how you want to see yourself and from what you are trying to achieve and be completely honest about this current chapter of your life. Let go of any defensiveness, any stories you tell yourself and any excuses, and be real. You have nothing to lose, but everything to gain.

The more open and honest you are with yourself, the more insight you'll have and the more change you can create. This is happening for you, not to you. It's an investment to the rest of your life. Get excited, because this is where all the magic is going to happen. So, let's learn about the different types of Food Jail and what we're working with.

Chapter 12
FOOD JAIL

Food Jail was a term I coined to explain the feeling of being trapped inside an eating disorder or cycle of eating disturbance, where body shape and weight is at the forefront of your mind. In a jail, you're confined to a small cell and your every move is dictated by a higher authority. You have no control. You're told when to go outside, when to eat and what to eat. When you've been especially bad, you're banished to solitary confinement. Jail is unpleasant, demeaning, isolating and depressing.

In Food Jail, you are confined in the prison of your mind. The higher authority is the eating disorder: the devil which dictates the rules you must live by. Breaking any of its dietary rules results in restriction, isolation and depletion.

What is a dietary rule?

A dietary rule is a rule made around eating and the food you eat. This might include dietary restraint such as attempting to restrict your food intake (how much you eat) or avoid certain food groups altogether (carbohydrates, for example).

Here are some common dietary rules created by an eating disturbance. How many can you relate to?

- You must start your day with exercise before you can eat.

- No milk in your coffee, because milk is dairy, and dairy makes you fat.

- You shouldn't eat carbs, because carbs make you fat—or you should have them early in the day.

- You must weigh all your food to the gram.

- You must eat the same food or food groups ('safe foods') every day and not deviate.

- You must log all your food on a calorie-tracking app.

- If friends invite you out for dinner, you must lie and say you had a big dinner before you came, and only drink tea.

- When you eat out, you must order your dressing on the side, or ask for no oil, or ask for super-healthy modifications to your meal.

- You must not leave the gym until you hit a certain goal, like 4 km or 1000 calories on the treadmill.

- You must exercise with a jumper on to 'promote thermogenesis' and sweat more. Plus, you ate too much last night so you need to hide that body.

- You must 'start your diet' tomorrow and vow to only eat salad, because you binged tonight.

- You cannot eat with a big spoon or plate because it means you're fat.

- You must eat very slowly and drink heaps of tea and water in between bites, because you eat too fast.

- You should avoid eating in front of others, as they will judge you.

- You must avoid sugar or processed food at all costs.

- You must not eat anything on your list of forbidden foods (like chocolate, bread, nuts and pasta).

- You must not drink alcohol; if you do, it must be vodka, lime and soda.

As you can imagine, rules were made to be broken.

Imagine yourself in a jail cell where the jail bars are made from breadsticks, chocolate, lollies and pastries. They're all you can see and all you can think about, all day long, while you feed yourself unsatisfying prison sludge. The only way to break free is to eat these bars of food that are constantly in your face, to get rid of them! This would give you a few moments of freedom, until the prison guards find out what you did and lock you up again.

You've been trying to resist the urge to be 'bad', however, and have spent your time rocking back and forth in the corner of your jail cell, probably doing sit-ups. Then, the jail guards go on break and stop monitoring your every move. You start to think about how hungry you are. You can't take it anymore. You feel so horrible, deprived and depressed. Just one bite of something sweet and satisfying might help. You tell yourself 'One bite!', but deep down you know it's never just one.

You have a mental battle back and forth that sounds a little like this:

> *'Go on—you deserve it, you've had a long day. You're so fat you might as well eat it anyway.'*

> *'No, I know that isn't true.'*

> *'Yes it is! You'll never be the person you want, so just give in!'*

You start pulling your hair, feeling upset and overwhelmed, and you pace up and down your cell, your heart rate rapid, afraid of losing control. So you do just that—you lose control and give in to the inner demon to shut it up.

You throw yourself at the bars of food like a wild animal going in for its prey. You are an animal: you don't even feel human when you're in this state. You begin ripping into anything you can find to satiate your starvation. You tear down bread, pasta, ice cream and anything else you can consume in record time, because soon the guards, the authority, will be back to put you in your place and take away your moment of perceived freedom. Until this happens, you are euphoric. Time doesn't exist, jail doesn't exist, people don't exist. All that exists is a state free of starvation, stress and feelings. You are in food euphoria.

Soon after, everything is consumed and the bars of food jail are gone. You lie there exhausted, depleted and humiliated. You want to curl up in a ball holding your painful abdomen, wondering whether life is even worth living like this.

Before you start crying, the guards come back and they drag you out for breaking down the cell bars. They tell you that you're a failure, worthless, and you can't stick to anything. You surrender, agreeing. You deserve to be punished; you deserve isolation. You're moved to a maximum security cell with no bars, no windows, no light and no human interaction. You don't know when your next meal will be, but it doesn't matter, because you don't deserve it. This is restriction mode.

Does any of this sound familiar? If it does, you are not alone. This was me. For nine years.

Chapter 13

EATING DISORDERS

Up to here, I've talked a lot about one of my own personal demons: bulimia. This might not be your issue. You might not make yourself vomit, and you might be within a healthy weight range—but that doesn't mean you have a healthy relationship with food, yourself or your body. In fact, who does? Think of three people you know: I bet one of them is preoccupied with being thinner or losing weight, or isn't happy with their appearance. No-one's perfect, but if you find you spend the majority of your life and time thinking about food and how you look, you can change this. You just have to want to try.

Alternatively, you might be reading this book because you suspect that someone you know might have a problem. In this chapter, I'll explain a range of eating disorders so you can start to understand the different types. Eating disorders are, of course, considered to be a category of mental health condition. To determine if someone has a mental health condition, psychologists often use a book called the *Diagnostic and Statistical Manual of Mental Disorders (DSM)*. After careful assessment, if a client meets a certain set of criteria, they might meet a diagnosis for a mental health disorder.

More often than not, however, a client will meet some of the diagnostic criteria in the DSM, but not all of them. In the fourth edition of the DSM, the DSM-IV, the diagnostic term which was applied when an individual's symptoms caused significant distress but did not neatly fit within the criteria of any specific eating disorder was 'Eating Disorder Not Otherwise Specified' (EDNOS). As online journal *Eating Disorders Review* reports, EDNOS was the most common eating disorder in 2012, with approximately 40 to 60 per cent of cases seen at specialist centres falling into this category.

The latest version of the DSM is the fifth edition, known as the DSM-5, and there have been some changes to the diagnostic criteria for eating disorders. EDNOS is now referred to as 'Other Specified Feeding or Eating Disorder' or OSFED.

The DSM-5 now lists six specific feeding and eating disorders, apart from OSFED:

- pica disorder

- rumination disorder

- avoidant/restrictive food intake disorder

- anorexia nervosa

- bulimia nervosa

- binge-eating disorder.

Let's look at each of these in turn, and the health impacts associated with them. I'll also cover body dysmorphic disorder, which isn't an eating disorder but is highly relevant. If you or someone you know presents with any of these, I strongly recommend getting professional help. Note that I've summarised the disorders: if you would like to understand the full diagnostic criteria of a particular disorder, please refer to the DSM-5 or talk to a mental health professional.

Pica disorder

You might have watched the television series My Strange Addiction, in which you see people eating chalk or baby wipes. This is pica disorder – when people ingest substances that aren't food. Usually this stems from a deep psychological trauma that has led the person to find comfort in eating this particular item and become attached to it. The disorder is defined as the eating of non-nutritive, non-food substances over a period of at least a month.

Pica disorder can lead to malnutrition and, in extreme cases, lead poisoning from eating soil or paint with lead in it.

Rumination disorder

Rumination disorder is when food is repeatedly regurgitated and this behaviour lasts for at least a month. The regurgitated food might be re-chewed, re-swallowed or spat out.

When I overate, I would sometimes bring food up without even trying because of how often I made myself vomit. It becomes an automatic action, and that's what rumination disorder is.

Avoidant/restrictive food intake disorder

Think of the pickiest eater you know and times that by ten. People with avoidant/restrictive food intake disorder have extremely sensitive eating habits or feeding patterns. They avoid eating based on food's sensory characteristics (for example, the 'furriness' of broccoli) and this perpetuates a lack of interest in eating. This disorder often results in significant nutrition and health deficiencies, as well as failure to gain weight (especially in children).

Anorexia nervosa

Anorexia nervosa is characterised by being severely underweight as a consequence of restricting food and energy intake. Individuals with anorexia have an intense fear of gaining weight and often fail to see their body as it really is.

There are two types of anorexia. The first is the restricting type—where the person restricts their food intake but has not engaged in bingeing or purging over the past three months. The second type is the binge-eating/purging type, where the individual has engaged in binge-eating and purging behaviour within the past three months. (The difference between this type of anorexia and bulimia is that the anorexic is severely underweight due to overall calorie restriction, whereas a bulimic may be a normal or higher weight.)

Anorexia nervosa is the most fatal mental disorder, as it's a medical disorder as well as a psychological one. A 2011 analysis by four researchers (Jon Arcelus, Alex Mitchell, Jackie Wales and Soren Nielsen) of 36 different studies indicated that only one in three victims of anorexia nervosa will fully recover and that the mortality rate is 10 per cent of sufferers. Death is usually due to starvation and metabolic collapse, but can also be from suicide. For this reason, sufferers need a team of professionals to help with treatment-planning and intervention.

Anorexia nervosa and avoidant/restrictive food intake disorder have the same health impacts; let's look at each of these in turn.

Cardiovascular impact

Restricting calories means that your body isn't getting enough nutrients and will start to break down your muscle. Your heart, one of the most important muscles, is negatively affected and your pulse and blood pressure will drop as the heart has less energy to pump blood around the body. This can lead to heart failure.

Gastrointestinal impact

If an individual is restricting food or purging, they'll experience slowed digestion, known as 'gastroparesis'. If they're vomiting on a regular basis and hindering the absorption of nutrients, gastroparesis can lead to:

- abdominal pain and bloating

- nausea

- blood-sugar fluctuations

- blocked intestines from solid masses of undigested food

- bacterial infections

- feeling full after eating only small amounts of food

- stomach ulcers.

The person will also experience constipation caused by two factors:

1. inadequate food intake, as there is not enough food in the intestine for the body to attempt to eliminate

2. weak intestines, as long-term inadequate nutrition weakens the muscles of the intestines, leaving them without the strength to propel digested food out of the body.

Neurological impact

Our brain uses one-fifth of the calories we consume, so dieting, fasting, self-starvation and erratic eating prevent the brain from getting the energy it requires. This leads to obsession with food and difficulty concentrating, which then impacts work and relationships.

Also, your body's neurons (nerve cells) require an insulating, protective layer of lipids (fats) in order to be able to conduct electricity—in other words, to be able to conduct nerve signals to your brain. Inadequate fat intake can damage this protective layer and cause numbness and tingling in your hands, feet and other areas.

Endocrine impact

Your endocrine system produces your hormones, and if you don't consume enough fat and calories, your hormone levels can be impacted. More specifically, the sex hormones estrogen and testosterone are affected, along with thyroid hormones. Reduced sex hormones then impact menstruation, causing it to become irregular or stop completely. (Losing your period completely is known as 'amenorrhoea'.) In addition, lowered sex hormones can lead to bone loss—osteopenia and osteoporosis—and this increases the risk of broken bones.

Other health consequences

Here are a few more consequences of self-starvation:

- Dry skin and brittle hair that may fall out, due to low caloric and fat consumption.

- The growth of lanugo (fine, grey hair on the body), in an attempt by the body to conserve warmth.

- Reduction in the number of blood cells, which also decreases the number of infection-fighting white blood cells.

- Kidney failure from severe, prolonged dehydration.

Bulimia nervosa

Bulimia nervosa is an eating disorder which involves bingeing and then induced vomiting. Individuals with this disorder eat an enormous amount of food within a short period of time (say, two hours), and their behaviour is usually secretive. When bingeing, the person may feel that they cannot stop eating or have no control over the amount they're eating. They also base all their self-worth and how they see themselves on their body shape and weight.

Everyone binges every now and then: what separates a bulimic from the general population is the frequency of the binges and the compensatory behaviours that go with it. To be diagnosed with bulimia, you must have been engaging in both bingeing and purging behaviour on a weekly basis, on average, for three months.

People can be diagnosed with mild, moderate, severe or extreme bulimia nervosa, based on how often they engage in the inappropriate compensatory behaviours. Mild bulimia is an average of one to three episodes in a given week; moderate is four to seven episodes; severe is eight to thirteen episodes; and extreme is an average of fourteen or more episodes per week.

Bulimia nervosa has many health complications, which vary depending on how severe, frequent and prolonged the disorder is. Here are some of the common problems.

Emotional impact

Bulimia is 'highly comorbid' with other mental disorders—meaning that it's not uncommon for those who experience bulimia to also have a secondary disorder such as anxiety, depression or obsessive-compulsive disorder.

Bulimics may be moody and irritable due to lack of vitamins and constant obsession over food. Concealing their secret maintains a cycle of stress and anxiety, guilt, embarrassment and shame. There's also an increased risk that they'll self-harm or develop suicidal thoughts or behaviour, for example, to deal with the stress and their extremely unhealthy body image.

Gastrointestinal impact

The cycle of bingeing and purging takes a toll on a bulimic person's digestive system. The activity is physically demanding and often associated with fatigue and general weakness.

Vomit contains high levels of acid, which can cause tooth enamel erosion, tooth sensitivity and gum disease. The person may have a sore throat and stomach pain from repeated vomiting, and the high levels of acid can irritate or tear the oesophagus; cause heartburn and acid reflux; damage the intestines; and cause bloating, diarrhea or constipation.

Bowel movement is also affected by the abuse of laxatives, diuretics and diet pills. Constant use of these products can make it difficult or even impossible to have a bowel movement without them, and over-strained bowel movements can result in haemorrhoids. The products can also damage the kidneys.

Cardiovascular impact

Dehydration as a result of frequent purging can impact the balance of electrolytes (potassium, magnesium and sodium) in the body and put strain on the heart. This can lead to an irregular heartbeat, known as 'arrhythmia', and in extreme cases, a weakened heart muscle or heart failure. Bulimia can also cause low blood pressure, a weak pulse and anaemia.

Endocrine system impact

Nutritional deficiencies caused by bulimia can lead to hormone imbalance, which can then affect the menstrual cycle. This can be impacted or stop completely, as ovaries no longer release eggs.

Integumentary system impact

The integumentary system includes your hair, skin and nails. Dehydration resulting from frequent purging leaves your body without enough water to replenish your hair: the result is often frizzy and dry hair, and in extreme cases, hair loss. Similarly, dehydration leads to dry, scaly and rough skin and also brittle nails.

Other health issues

Bulimics who constantly use their fingers to initiate purging may develop what's called 'Russell's sign' (named after British psychiatrist Gerald Russell)—calluses on the knuckles or back of the hand. These develop from repeatedly inducing vomiting over a period of time; often, the bulimic will then start using a plastic object instead of their fingers, to avoid leaving clues for others so they can keep the eating disorder secret.

The acidity in vomit can also scar the skin on fingers and hands, and as vomiting is a vigorous process, it can even rupture blood vessels in the eyes.

Another noticeable sign is referred to as 'chipmunk cheek syndrome' or 'bulimia cheeks'—enlarged or swollen cheeks caused by inflammation of the parotid tissue and swelling of the largest salivary glands. The parotid glands, in the back of the mouth, are responsible for secreting saliva into the mouth to assist with chewing, swallowing and digesting food. When you're bulimic and are constantly inducing vomiting, these glands become swollen, sore and irritated.

The severity of the swelling depends on the frequency of the purging behaviour and will only decrease once the purging behaviour stops completely. As you can imagine, having 'puffy cheeks' is quite distressing for an individual who has an eating disorder and is already obsessed with body image and wanting to be perceived as skinny.

Binge-eating disorder

Binge-eating disorder (BED) is sometimes called 'emotional eating', 'compulsive overeating' or 'food addiction'. As with bulimia nervosa, it involves repeated episodes of excessive eating over a short period. The food consumption continues to the point of discomfort; the individual feels they cannot stop or control how much they're eating and feels ashamed and guilty.

Bingeing can result in weight gain, but the person doesn't have to be overweight to have BED. The difference between BED and bulimia is that in BED, the bingeing isn't associated with the ongoing use of inappropriate compensatory behaviours like purging, fasting or use of laxatives.

As with bulimia, BED also has mild, moderate, severe and extreme levels of severity based on the frequency of the episodes. The levels are the same as those for bulimia: mild is one to three binge-eating episodes a week, and so on.

There are many emotional and physical health consequences associated with BED, which are outlined below.

Emotional impact

After a binge, a person with BED feels shame, guilt, self-hatred, anxiety and depression.

Physical impact

People with this disorder may feel discomfort from being so full and experience gastrointestinal distress. Some individuals maintain a normal weight, but most are obese or overweight, and this is associated with further medical complications, such as cardiovascular disease, high blood pressure, high cholesterol, high triglycerides and adult-onset diabetes (type 2 diabetes). If the food they eat is high in fat, the person may also develop gout.

Social impact

A person's relationships, career, finances and social life may also be impacted by BED. They're likely to avoid social events, especially if they're overweight and embarrassed by this, and their finances may suffer if they're spending a lot of money on binge food. Taking days off work to recover from a bingeing or purging episode can have a negative effect on their career, as can avoiding work events involving food, such as lunch meetings or 'pizza Friday'.

Body dysmorphic disorder

As I mentioned, body dysmorphic disorder or 'BDD' isn't a feeding or eating disorder—it falls into the class of obsessive-compulsive and related disorders. However, I believe it's important to mention this disorder, as it can be a significant contributor to eating disorders.

BDD involves preoccupation with one or more perceived defects in your appearance—a big nose, for example—that are barely noticeable to other people, if they're noticeable at all. The person does a great deal of mirror-checking (or avoidance of the mirror) and goes to great lengths to mask the defect or seek reassurance from others about it to reduce their anxiety. Other common repetitive or ritualistic behaviours include excessive grooming and skin picking, and the person may also engage in repetitive mental acts such as comparing his or her appearance with that of others. The preoccupation with the defect or defects interferes with the person's ability to live a normal life in multiple areas of functioning (i.e. work, social and personal areas).

A subtype of BDD known as 'muscle dysmorphia' is more common in men. In muscle dysmorphia, the individual is preoccupied with the idea that his or her body is too small or insufficiently muscular.

When diagnosing BDD and planning treatment, we examine the amount of insight the individual has into their disorder. A person might believe, for example, that 'I look ugly' or 'I look deformed'. If they have good or fair insight, they recognise that the BDD beliefs are definitely or probably not true; if they have poor insight, they typically think that the BDD beliefs are probably true. Or, they could have absent or delusional insight, which means that they're completely convinced that their BDD beliefs are true. This can make treatment more challenging.

There are many health consequences associated with BDD, but the most significant is the high suicide rate. According to BDD specialist Scott Granet in his article 'Impact of BDD' on the International OCD Foundation website, 25 per cent of individuals with BDD will attempt to take their own life.

Sufferers are also highly likely to have depression, social anxiety and substance-use issues and to be under financial strain. The reason social anxiety and subsequent social isolation is so prominent in this disorder is that people with BDD believe they look disgusting, and their constant rumination about their perceived defect leaves them with little energy to engage with others. Similarly, constant fixation on their appearance affects their ability to concentrate well enough at work and school. The financial issues arise from the measures that these people take to 'correct' their perceived flaw. They'll spend thousands of dollars on plastic surgeons, for example, as they're convinced their appearance is the problem. They are unlikely to seek psychological help initially, and by the time they do, they may have had multiple unsuccessful surgeries, then further surgeries to 'fix' the previous surgeries.

————

After reading through this list of feeding and eating disorders and about BED, don't be upset if you think you might fit the criteria for a disorder. These categories simply assist professionals to put together a treatment plan to help you effectively.

If you could relate to some of the criteria for a disorder, but not all, you might be experiencing or have experienced what I refer to as an 'eating disturbance'. This is okay, and you are not alone!

No matter what you might be going through, there are strategies you can learn that will help you improve your quality of life. Before we go on to look at those strategies, however, I'd like to talk about an emerging condition named 'orthorexia'. This isn't a diagnosable disorder, but is receiving popular media attention.

Chapter 14

ORTHOREXIA

We all know that 'fitspo' or 'healthspo' Instagrammer who promotes a 'plant-based lifestyle' with absolutely no deviation ever. Have you ever felt guilty watching these people because you ate something processed? I know it sounds ridiculous, but they have a subconscious effect on us! I know when I saw these people's posts, I felt like I couldn't stick to anything; I thought they were superhuman and I was a failure.

It's great to be a conscious, healthy eater and to be aware of the nutritional quality of food, but individuals with orthorexia become extremely fixated on 'healthy eating' to the point that it's damaging to their wellbeing. Orthorexia commonly begins as an 'exuberant' interest in healthy eating that escalates in severity and intensity over time.

American physician Steven Bratman first coined the term 'orthorexia' in 1996—as a joke to convince one of his patients of the unnecessary degree to which her life focused on cutting out foods from her permitted list. At the time, Dr Bratman was working in alternative medicine, where 'healthy diets' were being explored as alternatives to medications. This approach, surprisingly, had many negative consequences for patients.

What does orthorexia look like today? It's not merely veganism, a gluten-free diet or a general appreciation for healthy eating. According to Dr Bratman in his article 'Healthy Eating vs. Orthorexia' (on orthorexia.com),

'Adopting a theory of healthy eating is NOT orthorexia'. It's when the choice to eat extremely 'clean' becomes a compulsion, and the individual is no longer free to make their own decisions when it comes to food. They're bound by their own food rules, and this focus comes at the cost of other areas of their life, with functioning in social, occupational and other areas significantly impacted.

The reason the orthorexic individual is so driven to adhere to their selected diet is because their dietary compliance is closely linked to their self-esteem. For this reason, any deviation is associated with negative feelings of guilt and shame. The irony is that the pursuit of healthy eating becomes an extremely unhealthy fixation.

Orthorexia isn't an official eating disorder, and there are no diagnostic criteria and limited studies on the condition, so it's difficult to know just how many people suffer with it. It's unclear whether it's an isolated disorder or part of an existing disorder such as anorexia or obsessive-compulsive disorder (OCD). The studies which have been completed show that orthorexia is highly comorbid with OCD—meaning that an individual is highly likely to have both conditions.

What are the signs of orthorexia?

If you or someone you know is exhibiting the following symptoms, they may be a victim of orthorexia and require professional help:

- always checking the labels on food items for their ingredients and nutritional value

- displaying a growing concern for the health of ingredients in a product

- cutting out a food group or number of food groups (for example, meat, sugar or dairy)

- showing an inability or inflexibility around eating anything but a narrow range of foods that are deemed 'healthy', 'pure' or 'unprocessed'

- having an unusual preoccupation and interest in the health of what others are eating

- spending a significant amount of time per day (hours) thinking about what food might be served at upcoming social gatherings or events

- displaying high levels of distress when 'safe' or 'healthy' foods aren't available

- obsessively following food and 'healthy lifestyle' accounts on Instagram and other social-media platforms.

They may or may not have body image concerns as well.

The health consequences of orthorexia can be severe; they're similar to those for anorexia, due to the restriction of the amount of food that is eaten and also the variety.

Orthorexia versus anorexia or bulimia

Orthorexia may actually be a disguise for other eating disorders such as anorexia and bulimia, as it presents a more socially acceptable way of staying thin. However, while the behaviours are very similar across orthorexia and other eating disorders such as bulimia and anorexia (i.e. dietary restriction, bingeing, purging, malnutrition and weight loss), there are significant differences.

The content of the belief system is what differentiates the disorders. Someone with orthorexia thinks about ideal health, physical purity, enhanced fitness and avoiding disease (Mulheim, 2019). Their belief system causes them to idolise 'superfoods', which they believe contain special health benefits, and to demonise or restrict any foods they perceive as unhealthy. They believe they're striving towards 'ultimate health' and it's not about losing weight or restricting calories.

On the other hand, individuals with anorexia or bulimia are fixated on weight loss and will restrict food based on calories, not on whether the food is healthy or not. So, for example, anorexics are commonly seen drinking Diet Coke, because it has very few calories—whereas an orthorexic would view Diet Coke as unhealthy due to all the chemicals in it.

The other main difference between orthorexia and other eating disorders is the feelings associated with it. Anorexics and bulimics feel extremely ashamed of their eating habits and behaviours, whereas orthorexics may glorify their 'health regimes' and attempt to persuade others to follow the same health beliefs.

While more research is needed into orthorexia, it's not to be taken lightly and is associated with many health risks.

In the next chapter, we'll go a step wider, into the more general population, and look at a phenomenon I call 'eating disturbance'.

67

Chapter 15

EATING DISTURBANCE

'Eating disturbance' is when food, body shape and weight consume or influence your everyday decisions, but you're able to function and maintain a relatively normal life. In other words, you participate in life and social activities, but have thoughts niggling at the back of your mind about what you 'should' eat or drink or how much you should exercise. Such thoughts influence your behaviour and have an impact on your feelings.

For example, you might feel guilty after eating dessert and not be able to shrug it off, because you 'should' be eating healthily. Consequently, you may 'punish' or 'redeem' yourself by going to the gym or reducing your calories or food intake the next day. You might even self-sabotage by continuing to eat unhealthily, because you feel like you've 'stuffed up' and there's no point in trying to be healthy. The bottom line is that food, image and body shape occupy your mind the majority of the time and your emotional state is determined by your compliance with dietary or exercise expectations. Whether you're happy, anxious or upset depends on the decisions you've made regarding your exercise and food that day.

I've created the following checklist for you to go through in order to see if you can relate to the concept of eating disturbance. If you answer yes to some of the questions, don't be alarmed. Eating disturbance occurs on a spectrum and we all fit somewhere along that spectrum—we all have some disturbance in our lives that we can work on. The first step is to be aware of these tendencies, so we can manage them more effectively.

Answer each question as honestly, openly and non-judgementally as possible. This is to help you!

Eating disturbance checklist

- ☐ Do you spend the majority of your time preoccupied with what you're going to eat today?

- ☐ Do you constantly mirror-check or look at your reflection in windows?

- ☐ When you look at yourself, do you always look at the same parts of your body (e.g. your stomach)?

- ☐ Are you fixated on an area of your body and whether you've 'lost weight' in this area (e.g. legs, arms, stomach, buttocks)?

- ☐ Do you put your worth into whether people are physically attracted to you, and does this mostly have to do with your weight, shape or size?

- ☐ Do you find yourself referring to food as 'good' or 'bad'? (For example, 'I ate so good today' or 'I ate so bad on the weekend'.)

- ☐ Do you say, 'I've eaten so bad today' and then go off the rails and eat unhealthy foods because you 'stuffed up', and decide to start again tomorrow?

- ☐ Do you experience guilt, shame or disappointment when you've eaten unhealthy foods, gone 'off track', binged or eaten more than you believe you should have?

- ☐ Do you avoid social situations so you can stay home and 'be healthy', but then you end up eating or bingeing on 'forbidden' foods anyway?

- ☐ Do the majority of your conversations with others revolve around weight, food, exercise and diet?

- ☐ Do you only want to catch up with friends if it involves 'going for walks' or 'having tea'?

☐ Are you on the latest 'keto' diet or '28-day challenge' and feel bad when you're not eating keto/paleo/vegan or undertaking some sort of fitness or health challenge?

If you answered yes to three or more of the questions and these behaviours occur on a regular basis, you will definitely benefit from the strategies I've developed. You may live a relatively normal life now, but you don't yet know just how happy and free you can be.

Food Freedom

Why do you think we feel so happy when we're on a holiday? Partly, it's because we're in a state of 'Food Freedom'—we set ourselves free from dietary restrictions. How often do you come home from a holiday thinking you need to 'lose the holiday weight' and subsequently get post-holiday blues?

Imagine experiencing the Food Freedom you have on holidays in your regular life, every day. Imagine being at a restaurant and ordering what you actually want to order, instead of what you feel you should order. Imagine being able to order your favourite dish with no guilt or nagging thoughts. Imagine ordering dessert and enjoying every mouthful, rather than thinking about how you'll have to 'work it off' tomorrow. You can do this—you just have to want to try to change. And I know you want change; otherwise, you wouldn't be reading this book.

When you're happy and free from Food Jail, your body will naturally start to change and you will feel and look the best you've ever felt. Your body will find where it's meant to be naturally. You won't binge on foods, because you won't be restricted from them.

When you're mentally free, you are physically and hormonally liberated. You're no longer harbouring elevated levels of unnecessary cortisol and adrenaline from being anxious, stressed and guilty about your food choices. You naturally experience more serotonin and dopamine, which are the feel-good hormones. When you're happy, you're healthy—not the other way around.

Have you ever considered that you don't need to worry about your body weight, shape or what you eat? Yes—you can stop worrying and not put on weight as a consequence, because I'm not talking about 'letting yourself go', either! If you pursue the way of life I've developed, you can and will have it all—the body, the confidence, the self-love and a healthy life—because you want it, not because you feel you need to have it.

Remember, no matter where you are in life, you can always grow, develop and change—you just have to be open to feedback from yourself and the universe. Just because you are functioning, have a good job and relationships and feel fine, that doesn't mean your relationship with food and body image can't be improved to elevate your life even more. Imagine what you could achieve, physically and mentally, if you were not investing as much time, energy, behaviour, brain power and emotion into body shape, weight and food.

Here are some more questions for you to reflect on:

If I didn't have to focus on shape, weight, food or body image:

- **What would I be doing with my time and energy?**

- **What would I be eating?**

- **Where would I go?**

- **What would I wear?**

- **What would I be thinking?**

- **What could I achieve?**

Take a day or two to reflect on this before you read on. I want you to think deeply and journal what thoughts, feelings and emotions come to mind. Be open, trust yourself and let preconceived notions go. You may think journalling or reflecting is not for you or is dorky, but it takes courage to let these notions go and give something different a try.

So, be courageous. You owe it to yourself. Now is your time.

———————

For those sceptics who are still not convinced, let's delve into the science of Food Jail and the mind–body connection.

Chapter 16

THE MIND–BODY CONNECTION

The research on food restriction shows that inhibiting your food intake has psychological consequences. Think about the last time you tried to go on a health kick or diet: were you sitting at your desk thinking about food? Were you daydreaming or even dreaming at night of eating doughnuts? I used to dream about food all the time—Sigmund Freud would interpret this as wish fulfilment of our subconscious desires.

Dieting and restriction leads to binges once food is available. This is outside of your control—your brain doesn't know when it's going to be fed again, so it's in survival mode. This is why individuals feel a 'loss of control' when they engage in a binge. Your brain is literally yelling, 'FOOD, NOW!' It will usually go for the foods that give you the quickest energy boost; this is the reason people binge on carbohydrates and sugary foods. Bingeing isn't your fault, it's your brain and body trying to survive.

Food restriction also manifests psychologically in the form of obsessing about food. Examples of this include:

- looking at the clock and counting down the minutes until your next meal

- increased emotional responsiveness (e.g. feeling 'hangry' = angry due to being hungry)

- dysphoria (depressive mood)

- distractibility.

Ever felt you can't concentrate when you haven't eaten properly? This is a psychological consequence of food restriction.

Let's move on to hormones and specifically, serotonin. Serotonin is a feel-good hormone that regulates mood, appetite and sleep. What you might not know is that the majority of your serotonin is produced in your gastrointestinal tract, which is lined with a hundred million nerve cells (i.e. neurons). What this means is that your digestive system isn't just digesting food, it's also guiding your emotions. The reason we have expressions like 'butterflies in the stomach' is because the gastrointestinal tract is sensitive to emotion. Feelings such as anger, anxiety and joy can all trigger symptoms in the gut.

As you go about your day-to-day life, your gut produces chemicals that your brain uses to regulate mental processes such as memory, learning and mood. It also works the other way: when your mood is negative—you're stressed because you ate a loaf of bread, for example—your hormones can suppress beneficial bacteria in your gut and influence how your brain and intestines function.

Your immune system also plays a part in how your gut and brain communicate with one another. Research suggests that becoming low on beneficial bacteria in your gut from emotional stress or unhealthy eating could cause your immune system to produce chemicals that promote inflammation. This in turn can trigger mental health problems, such as depression! It's no wonder people who have eating disorders often also have anxiety and depression.

So, to use the earlier example, your (negative) perception of eating a loaf of bread would influence your mood, which would then influence your gut bacteria, which could then impact your learning, memory and overall engagement in life.

We must not see our body and brain as separate entities, and think, 'If only I can master my body, my brain will feel happy.' It's simply not true. The mind and body are interlinked, and we must be aware of this and kind to ourselves at all times in order to make lasting change.

Now that you're aware of the mind–body connection, I'm going to talk about something that not enough people talk about.

When it comes to eating disturbance and disorders, the focus is on eating behaviours, not on your body-related behaviour. This is why I developed the notion of 'body disturbance'. It's a term that brings awareness to how our mind can engage in body-checking activities we may not consciously be aware of. These activities magnify our dissatisfaction with our bodies and influence how we feel—and this, of course, encourages dieting behaviour and thus maintains dissatisfaction with your body.

Chapter 17

BODY DISTURBANCE

Do you purposefully walk past mirrors or windows to catch a sneaky peek of how you look? Or do you go to great effort to avoid seeing your body? Some of us switch between the two.

This is body disturbance: it's real and it's serious. It's one of the most common clinical features attributed to eating disorders and eating disturbance, and many of us don't even realise just how much we are influenced by it.

Your body disturbance is linked to your body image and is therefore sometimes called 'body image disturbance'. 'Body image' refers to how people see themselves and their body. A negative or distorted body image is when people have an unrealistic view of their body: this is more common in women, but does affect men too. Body image starts to develop in early childhood. As you saw from my story, I had thoughts about my body image at the age of six! You start to develop perceptions of your body's attractiveness, functionality and acceptability at a young age, and this is often influenced by friends, coaches and family members.

What are the symptoms of body disturbance?

There are six main signs and symptoms of body disturbance:

1. preoccupation with bodily appearance

2. mood and feelings are determined or influenced by weight, shape and size

3. body-checking behaviour

4. mirror-checking

5. comparing yourself to others

6. avoidance of body-checking.

Let's look at each of these in turn.

Preoccupation with bodily appearance

During the adolescent years, being preoccupied with your appearance isn't unusual, but just how much is 'normal'? If someone is frequently commenting on their own shape and weight and comparing it to athletes, fitspos or models on TV and social media, there may be some body image disturbance. Questions such as 'Do I look fat/bloated?' and 'Are my arms too big?' might be indicative of an unhealthy preoccupation with weight, shape and size. How much time does the person spend looking in the mirror, at windows and other reflections and on the scales?

Mood is influenced by weight, shape and size

I'll be the first to admit that my mood for the day used to be determined by the scales and whether I was 'feeling fat'. (We'll discuss 'feeling fat' in the next chapter.) When I was having a 'skinny day', or a day when I felt my body 'looked good', I'd be happy and over the moon and I suddenly believed that all my dreams could come true. I'd feel like I was suddenly worthy and getting somewhere with all my hard work. If, on the other hand, I woke up bloated—which was often—I felt like a 'fat failure' and would feel crappy for the day.

I would never consider that 'my bloating' might be due to an allergic reaction: I didn't feel I deserved to be let off the hook by a dietary intolerance. I believed my bodily changes day to day were just me being fat and were my fault. I wasn't open to other options or ideas as to why my body didn't respond as I believed it should—if it didn't, it was my fault. You'll soon learn just how wrong and damaging this belief system was.

Is your mood influenced by how your body looks or how much it weighs? Do you place your happiness on this? If so, it might be time to rethink, as there are many other factors I've studied and witnessed first-hand which influence weight on a day-to-day basis. That's right—no matter how much you diet or train, you cannot influence changes in hydration and time of the month. You're tying your mood, wellbeing and the way you live your life every day into something you have no control over. It's time to take the power of your day back from your body, which is unreliable and inconsistent!

Body-checking behaviour

Body-checking is something that can happen subconsciously, without our awareness. It wasn't until I started to address my issues that I noticed I woke up every morning and pinched the fat on my stomach. What was I hoping to find out?

I've since had clients who sit in therapy with me tapping on their collarbones, circling their thumb and middle finger around their bicep or using both their hands to measure around their thighs. These are all types of body-checking behaviour which form part of body disturbance and almost become OCD behaviours. Individuals feel they need to perform the behaviour to temporarily reduce the anxiety they feel as part of the preoccupation with their weight, size and body shape.

Extreme forms of body-checking may involve taking pictures naked every day so you can compare your body to the day before.

Mirror-checking

Mirror- and reflection-checking also happens subconsciously. Have you counted how many times you've checked yourself in a mirror in one day? You might be alarmed! This is the action of looking at yourself in a mirror or reflection; usually, you scrutinise the part of your body you're most insecure about. Constant scrutiny will actually make that body part appear larger and 'worse' in your mind! This is explained more later in this chapter, and there's an exercise you can try at home to prove that what you see in the mirror isn't an accurate representation of your body.

Comparing yourself to others

Do you notice yourself comparing yourself to other people you pass on the street, or only to people you believe are skinnier or more attractive than you? I'm sure almost everyone you choose to observe is thinner than you... There's a reason for this which will be explained a bit later.

Body-checking avoidance

On the other side of the coin are body-checking avoiders. Do you go to massive lengths to avoid looking at your image? Do you wear baggy clothes to avoid having to deal with your body?

I once met a client who refused to have a mirror in their house. They became agoraphobic and refused to leave their house, because they'd spend up to three hours a day mirror-checking their outfit, body and image before they went somewhere. This was debilitating, so they removed mirrors altogether.

Becoming a frequent avoider of the sight of your body is just as detrimental to your wellbeing as being a frequent checker. While avoidance soothes your anxiety in the short term, it increases anxiety in the long term, so that when you're faced with a challenging situation, it becomes even harder to approach or manage.

I agree that weighing yourself daily (or very often) isn't beneficial, and people avoid the scales to reduce distress or discomfort; however, people who frequently avoid the scales may indirectly be feeding the problem. Frequent avoiders never give themselves a chance to find out that their fears are perhaps not true—that they aren't putting on weight. More often than not, your fears are worse than your reality, so knowing your weight can sometimes be useful to overcome the preoccupation with it. It's almost as though you desensitise yourself to the scale and it becomes just a number and not an emotional dictator.

Other types of body avoidance include not wearing clothes that show off the shape of your body and not shopping for clothes. Shopping avoidance was a massive one for me. I'd buy items such as protein powders and gym shoes to feel like I was shopping and to justify spending money on myself, because I was 'investing' into my ultimate body. However, even the thought of going into a shop and trying on clothes made me extremely stressed (unless I had lost weight)! This was especially so if I went shopping with someone who was also body-conscious.

Some individuals also avoid touching their own body or seeing themselves naked, as this causes too much anxiety. Finally, you might not even notice it, but some individuals with body disturbance avoid or have minimal physical contact with others. Due to dissatisfaction with their shape, they avoid hugging, kissing and intimacy, which can adversely affect relationships.

The cycle of body disturbance

The following diagram shows how the preoccupation with body shape and weight influences body disturbance (in the form of mirror- and body-checking) and how this reinforces the dissatisfaction with the self and encourages dieting.

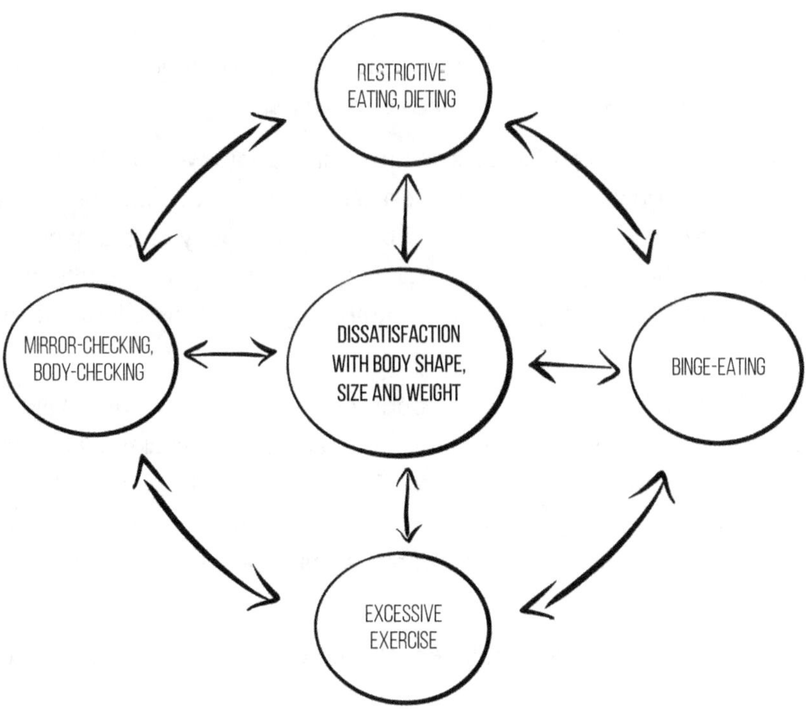

As you can see, it's a vicious cycle that doesn't end, unless we choose to end it.

How does body disturbance happen and why is it unhelpful?

Now you've learned about the types of body disturbance and what you might be doing without any conscious awareness of it, let's discuss why it happens, and why it's unhelpful and needs to stop.

Any form of body- or mirror-checking is unhelpful, because it reinforces dissatisfaction with body weight, shape and size and reinforces dieting. You know now that any form of dieting or restriction more often than not leads to a binge, so you can get what happens once you start dieting—you binge-eat, feel guilty and, alas, the Food Jail cycle continues.

Our bodies don't change much in minutes, or even hours, and when people scrutinise or focus on something, it actually appears worse. Have you ever tried something on quickly at a store, done a quick glance up and down, felt happy because you looked good, then went home and tried on the outfit, only to be horrified with how it looked? This is because when you tried it on at home, you scrutinised how the outfit looked in areas you're not happy with (your stomach or thighs, say).

A study was once conducted in which participants were instructed to scrutinise one part of their body for a certain time every day and, at the end of the week, rate whether they believed that body part changed at all. Despite the body part being exactly the same, the participants were convinced that the body part had gotten bigger over the course of the week!

Individuals with eating issues or body disturbances are more likely to focus on areas they don't like rather than areas they do like. When was the last time you looked in the mirror, focused on a part of your body that you like (your arms, say) and thought, 'Damn, my arms look good'? People generally focus on the part that 'wobbles', has cellulite or stretch marks, or 'looks fat'.

Let me ask you a question, and then tell you something that will blow your mind.

First, the question: have you ever had someone tell you about a car you'd never heard of, and the next minute you're seeing those cars everywhere?

This is due to your reticular activating system or RAS—a bundle of nerves at your brain stem that filters out unnecessary information so that the important information gets through. The RAS also seeks information that validates your beliefs. It will filter the world through the parameters you provide, and your beliefs shape these parameters. For example, if you think you're fat, you are going to look for and subsequently find fat areas on your body and this will then influence your actions, which might be restrictive eating and bingeing.

The RAS works subconsciously. Its job is to keep you safe, so it filters out what it thinks is unimportant. If you're in Food Jail, what you perceive as important and unimportant is obviously skewed, and so your RAS is constantly focused on information about body shape, weight and food.

People with eating disorders commonly have a distorted perception of themselves, too, especially when looking in the mirror or reflective surfaces. When you view something without context, especially if that item or body part has negative associations, it visually appears bigger to you. For example, if a spider ran across your bedroom floor and you had a phobia of spiders, you'd see it differently to someone who didn't have a phobia of spiders. A person without a phobia might think, 'Oh yuck, I better take care of that' and remove the spider. However, if you have a spider phobia, you would zoom in on the spider and tune out everything else around you, and this would make the spider appear much bigger because there's nothing to compare it to.

In the same way, when I looked at my 'fat stomach', I tuned out everything else and only saw my stomach, and this made it actually appear larger to me.

The mirror illusion

Remember that earlier, I told you we were going to do an exercise to prove that mirrors are not an accurate representation of reality? Here it is.

What you see in the mirror isn't an accurate reflection. When you look in a full-length mirror, the image looking back at you isn't actually the same size and height as you. The only way to understand this is to do an experiment: you need another person to help with this one.

The mirror illusion experiment

Step 1. Stand across the room from a full-length mirror, making sure your head and feet are visible in the mirror. You will see a full-length version of yourself in the mirror.

Step 2. Get your friend to stand next to the mirror with some sticky tape. Ask your friend to place sticky tape on the mirror at the point that marks the top of your head (tallest point) and a piece of sticky tape to mark where your feet are (lowest point).

Step 3. Measure the distance between the two pieces of tape and write down how tall your reflection was.

Here's an illustration.

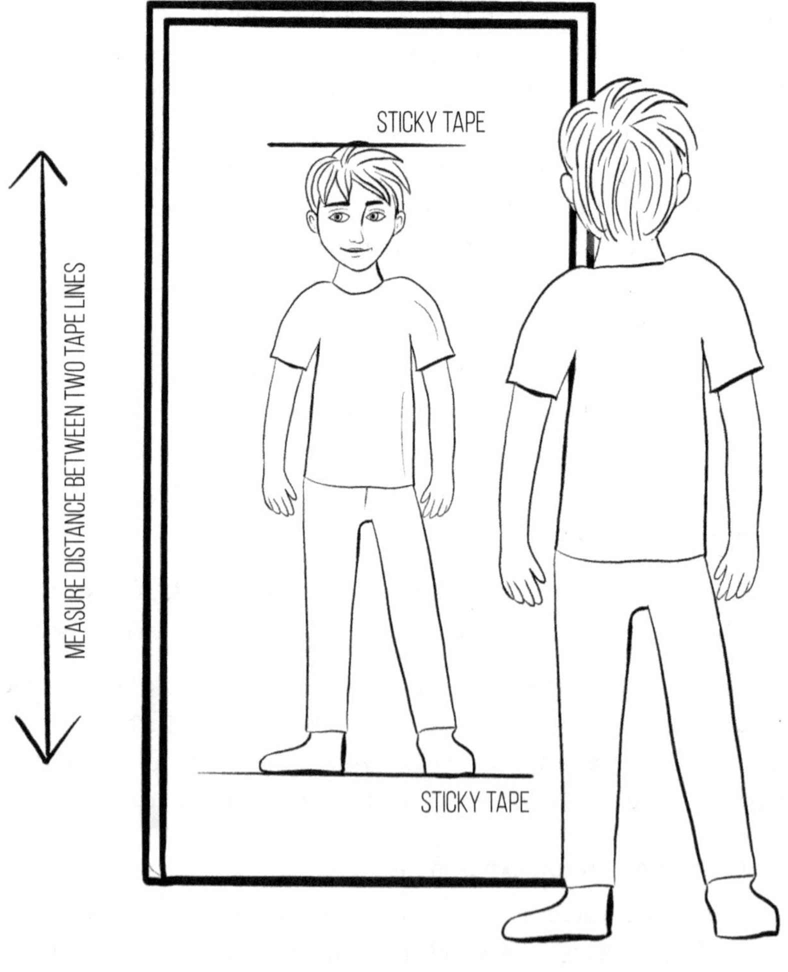

What you'll discover is that your reflection is nowhere near as tall as you: it is, in fact, a mini version of you. Yet, when you look in the mirror, you don't think, 'That's a mini version of me'—you perceive it as you. When you view yourself in the mirror, your brain converts or distorts the reflection so you 'see' a full-length version of yourself—because you're expecting to.

Similarly, when you gaze into the mirror at your 'fat stomach' you will 'see' a fat stomach—because you're expecting to! Your brain distorts the reflection so that you interpret it according to your expectations or fears about it (as in the case of the 'huge' spider).

As you can see, body disturbance has many aspects, and has the power to shape the way you feel and take control of your entire day. There is a type of Food Jail body disturbance that links the body and mind, and it's an almost universal experience. It's the phenomenon of 'feeling fat', and we'll discuss it in the next chapter.

Chapter 18

FEELING FAT

I've 'felt fat' and so have you. There's no denying this common experience, but what exactly does 'feeling fat' mean and just how detrimental is it to your wellbeing? The answer is that it's more damaging than you think, and I'm going to demonstrate why by asking you to do another little exercise:

Think of the last time you felt fat.

Go on, actually bring to mind the last time you had a 'fat day' or 'felt fat'. I want you to think about what you were doing on this day, or the night before, if you woke up feeling this way. Were you out with friends? Out for drinks? Or just having a quiet one at home with movies and snacks?

'Feeling fat' is more often reported by women than men, and often more frequently and intensely by individuals who have some eating or body disturbance. The problem is that people equate 'feeling fat' to being fat. No matter how they actually look, this phenomenon of 'feeling fat equals being fat' reinforces dissatisfaction with their body and, you know the drill—it encourages dieting.

Although there is little research on the 'feeling fat' phenomenon, the experience seems to change in intensity from day to day and even within a day. The current understanding is that feeling fat is often the result of mislabelling certain emotions, such as feeling hungover or groggy. 'Feeling fat' seems to be a broad umbrella term that can fit lots of other emotions in it, so that's why we tend to use it—but this is not useful.

Think about when you're feeling fat. Does it impact your thoughts and behaviour? Are you more likely to eat junk food because you don't feel good about yourself? Are you more likely to excessively exercise and restrict your eating for the day? Think about it, and write it down, because we're going to come back to this later. In Part Four, we'll explore ways to address this phenomenon which I use in my work with clients.

———

If you've got to this point in the book, well done. I know you're serious about making change. Now it's time for the fun to begin—in Parts Three and Four, you'll discover the world of Food Freedom.

PART THREE
FOOD FREEDOM IN YOUR MIND

This third part of this book is about escaping from Food Jail! We'll focus on changing your mindset by understanding how it works: learning about the mind, the power of thoughts and how to manage thoughts using cognitive (thought) strategies.

First, we master the mind, then in Part Four, we manage the behaviour.

Don't worry, I've got you!

Chapter 19

THE WAY OUT

Wow, you've come to Part Three of the book! I'm happy you've made it this far, as it shows one of two things: either you're super-motivated to make a change in your life, or this book is really good! In all seriousness, give thanks to yourself for giving yourself the time to read this and for investing in yourself.

We often get so caught up in what we 'should be doing' and feel guilty when we take time out to do something for ourselves. A big part of Food Freedom, of escaping the vicious cycle, is self-care, and just by reading up to here, you're already on the right track.

This part of the book will motivate you, inspire you and most of all make you see that it is possible to live a better quality of life—whatever that looks like for you.

What does success look like for you?

People have different goals, desired outcomes or visions, and one person's version of success might be completely different to someone else's. For one person, success might be trying new foods once a day; for another person, it might mean not beating themselves up over a binge and restricting the next day. What would success look like for you in this area of your life?

The other important aspect of success to remember is that it can differ from day to day, depending on your mood and circumstances in your life. On some days, success for one person might be getting out of bed in the morning. For another person, it might be having an uncomfortable conversation they've been putting off. It's important to know that your version and vision of success is yours and you never need to compare it to anyone else's. Depending on your mood, energy levels and other variables (including other people's actions or inaction), the meaning of success will change for you, and this is completely normal and okay.

I used to believe that success for me meant getting up super-early and completing a hundred different tasks on my list. I'd feel guilty and unproductive if I slept in or didn't finish my to-do list, which made me feel worse, even if I'd actually succeeded in other ways. Sleeping in, for example, meant that I wasn't tired and could function more effectively to complete the tasks on my list. It's all about perspective.

Now, on some days, success is just showing up to the gym and not completing my best effort. Success might be a day of meetings with people and getting none of my own work done. I've learned that, just because I'm not physically 'doing' doesn't mean I'm not investing in success in other ways. Success isn't always physical and tangible: it can be a mindset, it can be a meeting and it can be sleeping! As I said, it's different for everyone and different from day to day.

No matter how big or small your perceived success is, be proud of it and reward yourself. Positive reinforcement and self-compassion goes a lot further than punishment and self-ridicule.

It's also important to remember that there will be days where you don't feel like a success or that you accomplished much, but this isn't true. There's always something to be proud of each day, if you search hard enough. At the end of each day, I reflect on three things I am proud of—it could be connecting with a friend, completing a task or helping my mother. This gets me in a grateful and positive headspace before bed, rather than ruminating on all the tasks I have to do or didn't get done—which would keep me awake!

Progress over perfection and done is better than perfect!

Whatever success looks like for you, that's what we are going to work towards together. I am here with you every step of the way.

Better than okay

You picked up this book for a reason. Whether you're going through your own struggles or are looking out for someone else, or you're just interested in learning more—you've showed up because this is important to you and you want some sort of change in your life.

There are always ways you can enhance the quality of your life—and they all start with knowledge and the right mentor. There are tools and strategies that they don't teach in school that are very important for optimal functioning in all areas of life. Remember, too, just because you're 'functioning', that doesn't mean you're functioning optimally in your health, relationships, happiness or wellbeing. You deserve to wake up believing that you and your life are amazing, not just good. The 'Mind Food family' I've created with the people who've connected with me on social media doesn't settle for 'good'. We deserve more than that.

Despite being a mental health professional and having always been enthusiastic about living a healthy life, I continue to learn, so that I can function optimally. I might see naturopaths and acupuncturists to assist me with fatigue, for example, read resources or attend online professional-development seminars. There must be an area of your life that you'd like to improve—and guess what? The strategies I teach can be applied to any area—binge-eating urges, guilt, anxiety, depression, stress, relationship troubles or interpersonal conflict. In addition, research has shown that working on one area of your life has the side effect of naturally elevating other areas.

I've been trained in the most successful evidence-based therapies, and from each of those, I've hand-picked the most successful tools. I've tested the methods on myself and with hundreds of clients; I also utilise psychometric testing and measure change over time. I know my method works if the person is consistently applying the strategies. My methods work if you do.

I use my strategies daily to become a better person myself, because I'm constantly open to growth and feedback. Remember:

You are the most important project you will ever work on.

You don't magically change overnight, of course, and this is the reason some people never see long-lasting results: they stop trying before the method has had a chance to take effect. Technology has programmed us to crave immediate gratification. While this feels good in the moment, how often has seeking immediate gratification (by going on your phone, for example) distracted you and detracted from your goals and what you really want?

I teach you to evolve—evolve past the person you think you are and into the person you were destined to be. I give you the tools to facilitate your own evolution across minutes, hours, days, months and years.

Life isn't about changing who you are: it's about evolving into the ultimate self you desire to be.

You see, success and long-lasting change is about constantly learning and managing your day-to-day beliefs, behaviours and challenges. Small changes are what influence the bigger picture and are what will stop binge-eating or any other type of unhealthy habit or relationship with yourself.

Beyond on/off

Part of the reason that the world has an obesity epidemic is because people have been programmed to live in one or two modes: ON or OFF. You're either dieting or you're not. You're either eating healthy or you're not. This is why things like eight-week challenges gain so much traction: because people think change is about a time frame and method. A challenge can be a good kickstart, but to gain long-lasting results, you need long-lasting habits of the mind and body. You need evolution over time—this is why my clients work with me for years, not just over ten sessions on a mental health care plan. They might come in for help with a mental health concern, but they get addicted to making progress and our sessions turn into coaching and mentoring.

I wasn't put on this earth to just help people overcome mental health concerns—I want to take people all the way to achieve their full potential. In all areas of life.

In relation to eating disorders, the goal should not be, for example, to never binge again (in the case of people with bulimia). That's unrealistic and places so much pressure on a person, and when we feel pressure— we crumble. The goal is for your body shape, weight and binges to no longer be distressing to you. When distress starts to reduce, so does the unhealthy relationship with food; subsequently, the binges will reduce in frequency, intensity and duration as a side effect. I work 'backwards': while many professionals will give you strategies to stop disordered eating, in fact, the disordered eating is a symptom not the cause.

You'll learn that a binge isn't the end of the world and that you are okay. You'll learn that your response to obstacles is what's important, and this is where the real evolution occurs.

Mindset is magic

You might have picked this book up because you recognise that you've been locked in Food Jail at some point in your life, and you're over it. The penny finally dropped for me towards the end of 2015, when I asked myself, 'Will this cycle of binge-eating, dieting and stress actually ever end? If so, when?' If your answer to this question is, 'It'll end when I reach X weight or lose X kilos', you can bet that it won't end. It only ends when you say it does. You are in control—not the scales, not the food you eat or the clothes you wear.

I repeat—you are in control of how you feel and behave, and I'll teach you how to regain this control.

You'll live a happy life, free of sentences filled with 'shoulds' and 'musts'. 'I should exercise more', 'I must eat clean today', 'I should see my family more'. Such statements have been linked with feelings of guilt and anxiety, and although people use them in an attempt to motivate themselves, they actually have the opposite effect. Keep reading: I'll teach you how to get rid of 'must' and 'should' statements for good!

You can naturally come to love moving your body, nourishing your mind and thinking productive and effective thoughts. But you need to learn how to do this, because society and biology have led you to believe some pretty ridiculous thoughts about yourself and your capabilities.

It's time to stop poking yourself with a stick and start living a life in which you can have a doughnut and enjoy it 100 per cent, with no food guilt or resentment. In fact, you can have a doughnut and lose weight, just by changing your thoughts about it. Yes, that's right! My body only changed when I stopped trying to change my body and started to change my mindset instead. I lost weight and my body changed when I allowed myself to eat foods I'd been restricting myself from eating.

I was heading into my thirties when I recognised I'd spent all my teenage years and my twenties stressing about body image, excessive exercise and food restriction. I was so tired all the time. I'd watch my sister and her friends order desserts or coffee with milk in it and honestly believe I could never do the same if I wanted my dream body. I felt deprived all the time—but I still didn't have my dream body, and I wondered, what the hell was I even fighting for? Was this going to be the rest of my life? I decided right then and there that I'd earned the right to enjoy my thirties. And in my thirties, I've never been so healthy, happy, lean and fit.

The problem is not the food, it's the mindset. Why do some of the best gym and food programs not work? Because personal trainers and dieticians aren't psychologists and don't target mindset. This is why I've designed courses for personal trainers and people in the fitness industry—to help them help their clients with the emotional connection to food and themselves.

When you feel resentful, restricted or deprived, no diet in the world is going to work or to last. Your mind is the most powerful muscle of all, and will override any diet plan when it wants to. So the answer to success isn't external, in the latest diet plan or gym. The answer is inside you—you just need to learn how to activate it and harness it. You have the power within you, and I'm going to show you how to activate it.

It's time to get excited!

It's time to understand that there is nothing wrong with you the way you are now. However, it's absolutely okay to want to improve and move towards a healthier and fitter you—you deserve the chance to live an even better and more fulfilling life. That being said, self-improvement will only happen effectively if you're grateful for what you currently have. You can't build a double-storey house on a crumbling foundation.

You also need to realise that the problem isn't that you don't have any willpower or motivation. Motivation is a myth! No-one is motivated all the time. Sometimes (always) when my alarm goes off at 5 am, 6 am or even 7 am, I want to die. I feel so tired at times. However, I get up and go, because I've trained my mind and body to move, despite how I might feel—and you can too.

If your concerns are around eating, I want you to know that you are not the reason you can't seem to successfully 'lose weight' or stick to a diet. Your brain has become trapped in the vicious Food Jail cycle, and until you recognise and understand this cycle, you can't break it! You are not a failure, and you are good enough!

The chapters coming up offer a taste of my ultimate program—Food Freedom. They'll help you realise how your personal Food Jail works and how you can escape. Let's get started on enhancing your life!

Chapter 20

THE WHEEL OF LIFE

Awareness precedes change, as I've said before. This means that, in order to escape Food Jail, you first need to understand how your own internal prison operates. Once you know what you're dealing with, then you can work towards modifying it.

Eating can often happen without your conscious awareness, so I understand that what comes next is likely to be challenging for you. Remember, often what gets results is simple—but not easy. Grab your highlighter and get prepared to make some breakthroughs!

Let's look now at what I call 'the fundamental Wheel of Life'.

The Wheel of Life exercise

Here's my version of the Wheel of Life: the areas of life that I believe are the most important and integral to our functioning. In order to create change, we need to first become aware of how we feel about the different areas of our lives. Take a look at the wheel (on page 99) and see which area jumps out at you first that you think you'd like to change.

Many of us, I know, avoid exercises like this because we're afraid that we'll be disappointed. Remember, the only way to overcome fear is to do what makes us fearful. What's the worst that could happen?

If you want to step out of your comfort zone and evolve, now is the chance! You'll soon learn that it's not only your circumstances or situation which affect how you feel, but also the way you think about them.

How to do the exercise

Rate each area on the wheel out of 10, with 10 being 'excellent' and 'very satisfied' with that area of your life and 0 being 'non-existent' or 'extremely unsatisfied' with that area.

The areas are as follows:

- career
- finance
- personal growth
- health
- family
- relationships (romantic)
- social life
- mental health/mindset.

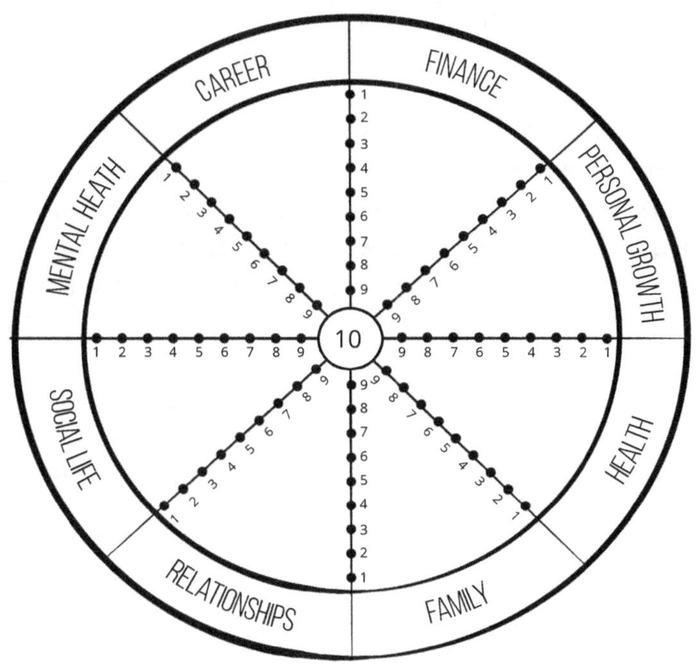

Here are some prompting questions to help get the juices flowing as you do the exercise. Take a notebook or a piece of paper now and don't hold back: write down exactly how you feel. The more honest and real you are, the better.

Career

On a scale of 1 to 10, how would you rate your satisfaction in your career? Are you happy with what you're doing and where your career is going? If not, what do you see yourself doing? What would be your dream career? What stops you from achieving this dream?

Finance

On a scale of 1 to 10, how would you rate your satisfaction in your finances? If you're not satisfied, why? What would make this number higher? What would need to change?

Personal growth

On a scale of 1 to 10, how would you rate your satisfaction with your personal development and growth? Do you feel you're investing time in growing yourself personally, professionally or in any other area of your life? This could involve reading books, listening to audiobooks or podcasts or attending seminars. What would an enhancement in this area look like?

Health

On a scale of 1 to 10, how would you rate your satisfaction with your health and physical body? These might be in conflict, and that's okay. Do you feel you nourish your body with the right foods and exercise? If not, what would your health look like if it was improved? How will you know when you're satisfied with this area?

Family

On a scale of 1 to 10, how would you rate your satisfaction with your relationships with your family? Is there anyone in particular you think about when you're reflecting on this? What would you like to see change? How would you like this area of your life to be?

Relationships (romantic)

On a scale of 1 to 10, how would you rate your satisfaction with your romantic relationships? If you're in a relationship, are you happy with it in general, with the intimacy and the physical connection? What areas of your romantic life do you want to see change in? If you're not in a relationship, what are you looking for in this area of your life?

Social life

On a scale of 1 to 10, how would you rate your satisfaction with your social life? What would you like to see change in this area? What would need to happen for you to rate this higher?

Mental health/mindset

This is where my Wheel of Life differs: I include mental health. On a scale of 1 to 10, how would you rate your mental health or mindset? Do you currently struggle with any mental health conditions? If so, what contributes to these problems? How are your mindset and mental health currently being managed? What makes you rate your mental health or mindset this number? What would need to happen for this number to change?

Barriers to success

After completing the exercise, take a break—you did really well. Then, I want you to consider: overall, what stops you from getting what you want? Think of three barriers to success you can identify and write them down now. Is it your circumstances, mindset or negative thoughts?

After you've completed this task, set some goals for what you want to see happen over the next three months.

Now, setting goals is great, but what people don't teach you is what to do when your thoughts get in the way of you taking action to achieve your goals. This is why people see such a great change when they work with me. I don't just 'motivate', I anticipate and help the client annihilate the things that will stop them from achieving their goals. We prepare for procrastination, negative beliefs and lack of motivation.

As a coach, psychologist and motivational speaker, I'm goal-driven and solution-focused and I will not stop until you have your desired outcome.

So, next we're going to focus on the number-one factor that takes you away from your goals—your thoughts.

Chapter 21

UNDERSTANDING YOUR THOUGHTS

This is probably the most important part of the book, where you'll learn the key to recognising your thoughts, feelings and behaviour. The strategy I'm about to teach you can be used to understand absolutely any emotion or behaviour in order to change it. I've used this technique with my clients for anxiety, depression, OCD, eating disorders, post-traumatic stress disorder, personality disorders and trauma. To explain the model, though, I'll be using the example of a Food Jail thinking pattern.

The ABCD model

To make it simple, I'm first going to break down the Food Jail cycle using the ABCD model. The ABCD model is based on the ABC model, which was developed by Aaron Beck as part of cognitive behavioural therapy—I've added the 'D'. In the model, 'A' stands for 'activating event', 'B' stands for 'beliefs', 'C' is for 'consequences' and 'D' is 'doing'.

A. The activating event

The 'activating event' is what triggers the Food Jail cycle—the thing that triggers you to feel upset, anxious or stressed about a given situation, such as breaking your healthy eating rules and having a doughnut.

Now, an activating event can be an actual event, something that happened—like eating a doughnut or a block of chocolate—or it can be a thought or even an image. For example, just thinking, 'I'm fat', or visualising yourself in a negative way (or seeing something bad happen), can trigger you to feel negative emotions and thoughts. We all experience this.

B. The beliefs

Next come your beliefs or thoughts about the activating event—what you're thinking in relation to that event. For example, if your activating event was eating chocolate when you're trying to eat clean, your beliefs or thoughts might be:

- 'I can't stick to anything.'

- 'I'm such a failure.'

- 'I've ruined the day, I might as well binge.'

C. The consequences

The 'C' in the model stands for the consequences—how you're feeling as a result of A and B. This includes how you feel psychologically (i.e. your emotions), physically (i.e. your visible body responses, such as sweating) and physiologically (such as having a fast-beating heart or shallow breathing). Here are a few examples of consequences you might feel:

- Psychologically or emotionally, you might feel depressed, anxious or stressed.

- Physically, you might experience shaking, sweating or going red in the face.

- Physiologically, you might experience a tight chest, a knot in your stomach, shallow breathing or rapid heart rate.

D. The do

The 'D' stands for 'do'—as in, what did you do as a result of A,B and C? It's the behaviour you engaged in. Let's say your Food Jail cycle went like this, for example:

- **A**ctivating event—eating chocolate

- **B**elief—'I've stuffed up my clean eating, I might as well eat crap'

- **C**onsequence—feeling guilty and anxious.

What might the 'Do', your behaviour, be? Perhaps it might be:

- eating a whole block of chocolate

- going on a binge

- shutting down and cancelling upcoming social events

- restricting your intake the next day

- excessive exercise.

The following diagram shows the vicious cycle of the ABCD model: how situations trigger thoughts, which trigger feelings, which in turn trigger behaviour. Our choice of behaviour can then either leave us feeling guilty and depressed or empowered and in control. Usually, it is our thoughts which determine which pathway we take from there.

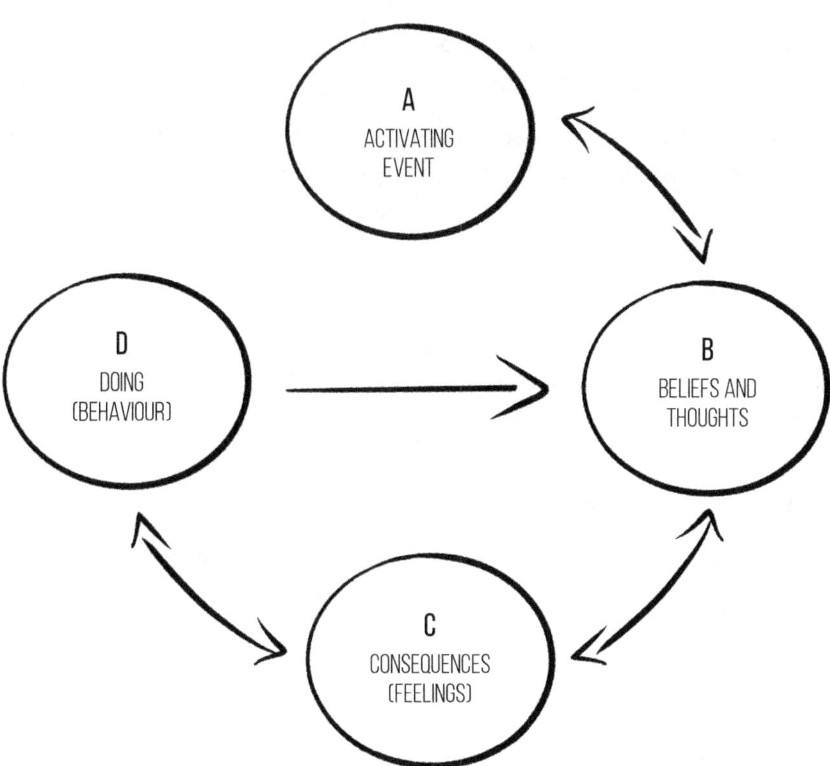

Now that you understand how your feelings and behaviour are interlinked, it's time to understand your mind specifically and work to retrain that brain!

We're going to map out what is going on for you the next time you feel upset, overwhelmed, anxious or any other strong emotion. The best time to complete this exercise is in at the time or just after it's happened, as that's when you'll get the most true and accurate data. This can be more difficult than it seems. When we feel an uncomfortable emotion, the first thing we want to do is get rid of it—this is programmed inside of us from childhood. So, for this exercise to work, you need to be aware of the urge to avoid strong emotions and not to let this urge overpower you and prevent you writing down your true feelings.

As time passes, we tend to talk ourselves out of how much a situation affected us. This is because as time passes, the emotional mind settles down and processing takes place, especially during sleep. This processing reduces the perceived impact of the situation on us and we may start to think of it differently. However, this doesn't mean that we've resolved the problem or understand it. It only means that our reaction to it has become less intense over time.

With Food Jail behaviour specifically, I know how tempting it is to want to 'start fresh' and not think about what happened following a binge. I know what it's like to feel the shame and guilt associated with the binge, and the perception of failure. I know the last thing you want to do is reflect on what happened.

I want you to remember this—a breakdown leads to a breakthrough. The ABCD exercise will help you understand yourself on a deeper level. Let's go through the exercise in more detail now.

Identifying the activating event

The next time you're feeling low or anxious, or feeling any strong negative emotion, grab your notepad or open a note-taking app in your phone. I want you to ask yourself:

- What is the activating event?

- What triggered how I'm feeling right now?

I know you may be feeling upset, but just take a step back from this and notice what you're feeling and thinking and what triggered it all. There's no right or wrong answer, so just write down whatever feelings come up for you.

Now, it's likely that thoughts might come up when you're trying to think of feelings. This is okay—write them down. Keep in mind, though, the goal is to recognise the difference between thoughts and feelings. We'll be separating thoughts and feelings a bit further along in the exercise, but for now, your goal is to get whatever's going on in your head onto paper.

If you struggle to identify the activating event, also ask yourself:

- **When did I start feeling this way?**

- **What was I doing just before I started feeling this way?**

Don't forget that the activating event can be a situation, a thought about something or even a feeling or an image you visualised.

A tip to help you identify your activating event
Instead of being 'in that emotion', step back and try to curiously analyse what started the emotion or triggered it. It might take time to get the hang of this, but with practice you'll become your own psychologist in this!

Identifying your beliefs

Once you've identified what the activating event was, it's time to identify the beliefs—what you're thinking as a result of the activating event. Ask yourself:

- What am I thinking right now?

- What thoughts are going through my head?

- What do I believe about myself at this moment?

- What do these thoughts say about me?

- What do these thoughts mean to me?

This may be confronting, as you may discover some thoughts you weren't ready to hear. Stay with it and write down whatever comes up, no matter how intense, irrational or ridiculous your thoughts may seem. When you are in a heightened state, your thoughts are more likely to be irrational, yet knowing this won't stop you believing them and being impacted by them. The point is just to get them on paper.

Identifying the consequences

Now let's discover the consequences—how you feel as a result of the activating event and the beliefs. Try asking yourself:

- What am I feeling right now?

- Where do I feel this in my body?

- What emotion am I feeling?

- Do I have any physical symptoms, such as sweating?

- Do I have any physiological symptoms, such as a pounding heart or shallow breathing?

Write down any feelings you're experiencing and break them down into psychological feelings (feelings you can't see, such as being upset, sad or anxious) and physical or physiological feelings (sensations inside and outside your body, such as feeling sick, having a knot in your stomach, heart racing, sweating or shallow breathing).

I can't label my emotions!

If you find it hard to express or label your emotions, don't worry, you're not alone. With practice, you will get better at this. I've included the following emotion wheel to help you to develop your emotional library and find the words to describe how you feel.

Start from the middle of the wheel and try to identify your most basic, prominent feeling. Then work your way out to try to find more words to describe how you feel. This can help you develop a deeper understanding of what's going on in your internal world, and eventually you'll find themes emerging.

The emotion wheel

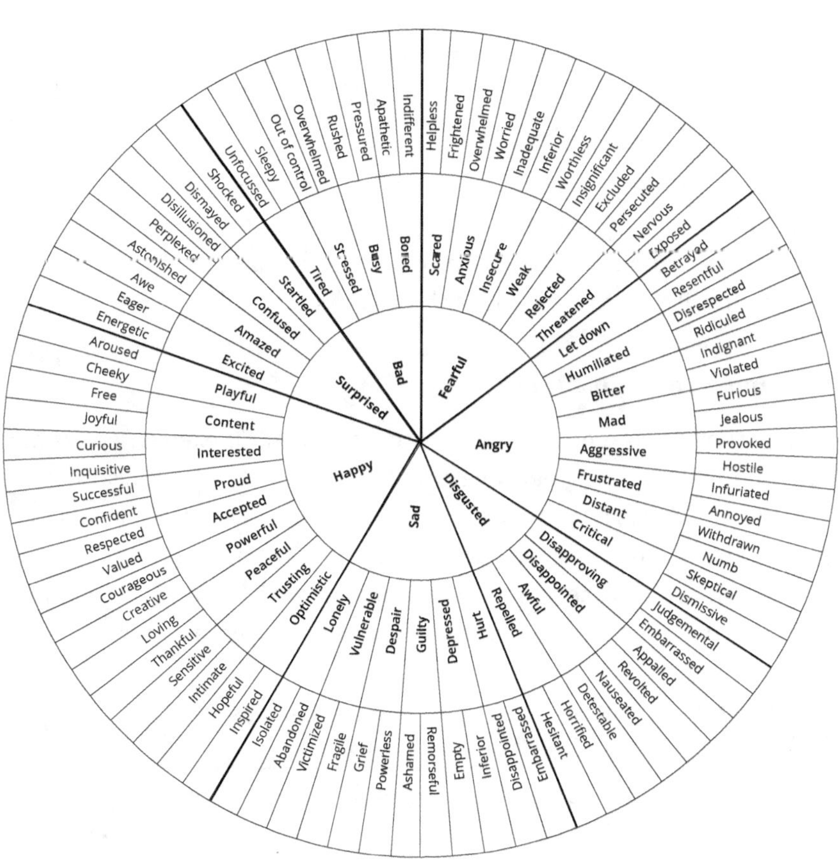

Identifying the 'doing'

Finally, it's time to identify the 'do'—the behaviour. What did you do as a result of the activating event, beliefs and consequent feelings? To identify your behaviour or your urge to behave a certain way following an incident, ask yourself the following questions:

- What did I do once this all happened? (Binge-eat, self-harm, call someone?)

- What did I feel like doing?

Sometimes what we want to do and what we actually do are two totally different things, and it's helpful to recognise this, as it can often show you're making progress over time.

Try to write down your actions in as much detail as possible, no matter how bad you might feel about them. Remember, this is to help you! If you're ashamed about your behaviour—please don't be! I promise the behaviour will change once you embrace my strategies.

Keeping a thought diary

It can be helpful to keep a log of your completed ABCD exercise each time you experience a strong negative emotion for a while—this is also known as a 'thought diary'. I don't want you to try to change anything: just notice your thoughts, feelings and behaviours and write them down. Following is a table that you can use as a template, with a row filled in as an example. Give it a go the next time something happens or you feel a strong emotion!

ACTIVATING EVENT	BELIEFS (THOUGHTS)	CONSEQUENCES (FEELINGS)	DO (BEHAVIOUR)
Being invited to a party.	*'No-one will talk to me.'* *'I'm going to look bad in what I wear.'* *'I won't fit in.'*	*Anxious* *Heart racing* *Sick feeling*	*Say I can't make it and avoid the party.* *Go to the party and drink excessively.*

Remember, what we measure, we can manage, but first we need data. Awareness precedes change! Once you've logged a couple of examples, you can move on to the next chapter to understand how it's all connected.

111

Chapter 22
THE B ⟶ C CONNECTION

One of the reasons I asked you to log your thoughts, feelings and behaviour in the previous chapter is that you, me and the rest of society are led to believe that it's the activating event that causes the consequences and the subsequent behaviour. To put it another way, people believe that:

Events → Negative feelings → Negative behaviour

People then think they need to avoid the activating event to solve the problem and reduce the negative feelings. For example, they might think 'eating a piece of chocolate' (the activating event) causes them to feel guilty, which causes them to binge (the behaviour). Or they might think it's 'parties' (the activating events) that make them anxious, so they avoid going to parties. They make a false connection between the activating event, feelings and the behaviour, and may believe, for example:

- 'If I just don't eat chocolate, then I won't feel guilty and a binge won't happen.'

- 'If I just don't go to parties, then I won't feel anxious.'

While this might work in the short term, it's not an effective management strategy long term, as you can't avoid chocolate and parties forever. The moment you do decide to have chocolate or go to a party, the anxiety and guilt is going to be intensified.

The truth is that activating events don't cause consequences (behaviour)—if they did, everyone would have the same behaviour. Think about it: how can two people experience the exact same activating event, but have completely different feelings about it and different behaviours?

The answer is simple and will change your life:

It's the thoughts and beliefs about the activating event that make all the difference.

Let's look an example to demonstrate how two people in the exact same situation can have a completely different experience because their thoughts and beliefs are different. The example activating event is 'being invited to a social event'.

Meet Jo (male) and Flo (female). They work in the same corporate office and have worked at the company for the same amount of time. Everyone in the office likes both Jo and Flo. Let's see what the ABCD model brings up for each of them when they're invited to after-work drinks with the rest of the office:

PERSON	ACTIVATING EVENT	BELIEFS (THOUGHTS)	CONSEQUENCES (FEELINGS)	DO (BEHAVIOUR)
Jo	Invitation to after-work drinks.	'This is going to be fun.' 'I can't wait to talk about the tennis.' 'We should get together more often.' 'I can't wait to go!'	Happy Excited Motivated	Goes to the party. Engages with people. Talks about how good it was the next day.
Flo	Invitation to after-work drinks.	'I don't have anything to wear and everyone else always looks so nice.' 'I think they only invited me out of pity.' 'I never have anything interesting to say.' 'They'll probably think I'm boring.' 'I should just say I feel sick and not go.'	Worried Anxious Apprehensive Sick in the stomach Heart racing	Spends a lot of time worrying about how it will go and thinking about how she can get out of it. Comes up with an excuse not to go (avoidance).

As you can see, the 'Activating event' column is the same for both people. However, notice the difference in the 'beliefs' column? Jo and Flo have a completely different set of thoughts about the activating event, and these influence their feelings and subsequently their behaviour.

Jo has positive thoughts: he's excited about the event and as a result feels happy and motivated about going. He attends and has fun, and this reinforces his belief that after-work drinks are a good idea—he's likely to go again.

Flo, on the other hand, thinks negatively about the event. Her thoughts are focused on what people may think of her, despite having no evidence to support this. Her negative beliefs about the event make her feel anxious and apprehensive about going, and this affects her behaviour: she avoids the event to temporarily relieve her anxiety and distress. This works in the short term, but it actually exacerbates her anxiety in the long term, not only for social events but also for anything that triggers her to think and feel in the same manner.

Avoidance perpetuates anxiety

You see, the mistake you've been making, and which I made for years, is believing that you have to change either the activating event (the situation) or the behaviour. For example, I believed I had to stop eating certain foods (the activating event) to avoid 'triggering' a binge-eating episode. I also thought I had to stop bingeing to change how I felt (the 'C' consequences, which were guilt and shame). At no point did I realise it was my thoughts that caused my emotional turmoil and reinforced my bingeing behaviour.

In the earlier example, Flo avoided the work social events because she believed that 'parties' make her anxious. This might be true, but it's not the complete truth or the answer to the problem.

Avoidance perpetuates anxiety. While it reduces anxiety short term, it actually maintains anxiety long term and makes it even harder to overcome. To return to a Food Jail example, while not eating chocolate in the short term might prevent a binge for a day or two, it's not realistic or sustainable, so avoiding chocolate is not the solution to avoiding a binge.

The solution is to change the thoughts and beliefs around eating chocolate. I believed that 'If only I could eat clean, then I wouldn't binge'—but it was the preoccupation with eating clean that actually led me to binge!

Restriction leads to binge!

If the Food Jail theory were that eating chocolate or junk food makes you binge—then why doesn't everyone who eats chocolate or junk food binge? How can thin, fit and average-bodied people who eat chocolate and junk food and don't binge exist? And no, it's not due to their metabolism or willpower!

The difference is our thought patterns and beliefs when it comes to eating these foods.

I know you, and how unkind you can be to yourself when you eat a food that you perceive you don't deserve or need. I know your mothers all too well, when they comment on what you're eating and how you're 'looking', and I know how this reinforces your negative beliefs about food and your body image.

While situations can trigger us to think and feel a certain way, the situations aren't the thing we need to change for long-lasting success and happiness—it's our thoughts and beliefs. Our beliefs about a situation lead to consequences (our feelings). This is the B→C connection. Your beliefs or thoughts about an activating event are what control your behaviour. They dictate how you feel and subsequently how you behave. In other words, the B→C connection is:

Beliefs → Negative feelings → Negative behaviour

Chapter 23

THOUGHTS VS BELIEFS

You might be wondering at this point, 'How do I know the difference between my thoughts and beliefs?' We've talked about them a lot as part of the ABCD model and in relation to the B→C connection.

The difference between a thought and a belief is that you may have thousands of thoughts going through your head each day— in fact, up to 70,000! However, your thoughts don't have any power of influence on you or your life, unless you emotionally connect to them via your beliefs. A 'core belief' is what makes a thought seem real, even though it may not be.

Have you ever had an irrational or silly thought and been able to shake it off, but other times you have a thought that bothers you or affects how you feel? This latter thought is likely to be connected to a core belief. You may even recognise that the thought is irrational or not true, but it still affects you.

Thoughts connected to core beliefs can manifest into actions or feelings. Only the thoughts connected to strong beliefs and emotions will affect your behaviour and ultimately your life.

For example, say I came into the world with an unconscious belief that the world is a dangerous place. Despite having no conscious thought that the world is dangerous, as long as that belief is operating in my subconscious mind, I'd manifest that I was unsafe. That belief would be working all the time in the background and could be triggered at any time. This might influence my behaviour; for example, feeling too scared to go out late at night.

Let me make this relatable. Say I come into this world with the unconscious belief that being thinner attracts more men. When I'm in a social situation and see a man looking at me, I might think that he's checking out my friend, who is thinner than I am. The situation triggered my subconscious belief to come to the surface as a thought. Then, because I assume this man is looking at my friend and not me, I behave in a way that shows no interest towards him. He may, as a result, then go for my friend—reinforcing my core subconscious belief that being thinner attracts more men.

How do our core beliefs develop?

You may be thinking, 'But where do these core beliefs even come from?' It's your life experiences that shape your beliefs. Core beliefs form in your subconscious mind throughout your life, based on your upbringing, situations and life experience. If you grew up with a mother who dieted, for example, and was always trying to lose weight because she believed that being thinner meant being happier—this would become your subconscious belief too. This belief would then subconsciously result in thoughts such as, 'I really should lose weight', and then this would influence your actions and behaviour—you might, say, choose low-fat yogurt over full-fat at the supermarket.

Core beliefs are intertwined with how you think, act and feel on a daily basis. They impact your energy and emotions. The more emotion that's attached to a core belief, the more control it has over who you are, how you perceive the world and how you act.

The good news is, once you start to identify your ineffective thoughts and learn about your core beliefs using the ABCD tool, you can act to change them. Knowing your core beliefs and their triggers will enable you to change, challenge and restructure them. This will ultimately give you the power to control your mind, feelings and behaviour and get your life back.

By now, it should be clear that it's not your situations or behaviours you need to change—it's your thoughts and, ultimately, your core beliefs.

Your thoughts are not facts.

Focus on what's effective

Now, I'm not suggesting you should be positive all the time—that's unrealistic. It's about being effective. Yes, you might have binged on a block of chocolate, say, but is it effective to call yourself a big, fat failure? Labelling yourself this way based on a real event only maintains your dissatisfaction with your body and encourages dieting. And dieting then encourages bingeing, so all you're doing is feeding the vicious cycle of Food Jail.

Here's another example of being effective but realistic: you could acknowledge that thoughts such as 'Parties make me anxious' might actually make you anxious and lead to the thought that people think you're boring. Maybe what influenced the belief that people think you're boring is that once, in primary school, a friend called you boring. Even though this happened, it isn't useful to allow the belief to govern your life. It's not effective or useful to avoid parties because of this.

We must learn to recognise when our life experiences hijack our beliefs and reinforce avoidance. We must work on the deep problems—in this example, the core belief that 'People think I'm boring'—and not just manage the symptom, which is the anxiety caused by parties.

Choose your hard

You might be thinking, 'This all sounds too difficult! It'll be too hard to change.'

Is this a core belief that comes up for you in other areas of your life? That it's all too hard and nothing will change? See how ineffective thoughts and core beliefs spread into multiple domains in your life? If this is you, make sure you read on, because I know you can change the thoughts which are holding you back from living an optimal life.

It's time to get deep and ask yourself, 'What are my core beliefs and what have they cost me over my life?' Have faulty thinking patterns cost you opportunities, potential friendships and relationships, career growth and happiness? You have one life, and it's time to start living it to the fullest and happiest, free from the mental prison that holds you back.

I'll teach you how to become a master of your mind, so you can control it rather than it controlling you! You'll see changes in your life that you never thought possible, because you can apply these strategies not only to your eating habits, but also to your relationships, family and career. You'll reach levels of pure happiness and joy you never imagined existed.

So: you've learned how to become aware of your thoughts. It's time to look deeper into the language and meaning you give these thoughts, and how to change them. Get ready—your life is about to change!

Chapter 24

IT'S TIME TO BECOME AWARE

Words are your world. There's so much research that supports this idea—that the words you say to yourself affect the way you think, feel and behave.

Think about a successful person who you look up to. Do they put themselves down? Can you imagine this person berating themselves out loud on a regular basis? Now think of someone you know who does talk themselves down a lot—what do you notice that's different about these two people's energy, aura and the way they carry themselves? (This second person could even be you, but all of that is about to change.)

'Self-talk' is the way you talk to yourself: your inner dialogue or internal voice. It's crucial to become aware of it and keep an eye on it, because it has a big impact on how you feel and act. If you often think negatively about yourself, this can drag you down—and when you're down, it can be really hard to get back up!

The words you say to yourself can have a big influence on what food you put in your mouth. For example, if you say to yourself, 'You're fat and you might as well eat that cake'—that isn't going to motivate you to feel happy and make the most effective decision. It will motivate you to eat the cake and feel guilty—even worse than you felt before.

'Food language' is a term I use with my clients to zoom in on their self-talk around food. This is such an important part of moving out of the vicious cycle of Food Jail and living a healthy, happy life. You need to think of words as the food or fuel for your mind. The words you feed your mind will have an impact on your emotional health, so choose healthy, effective self-talk—otherwise things will never change. After all, what are you gaining from speaking negatively about yourself?

What is your self-talk costing you?

Confidence, happiness, action and motivation—all of these come from within, not from outside, despite what you might think. Are you someone who thinks, 'I'll be confident when I achieve [insert external goal]', 'I'll be happy when [insert external object]' or 'I'll take action when [insert ideal situation and circumstance]'? If so, you're giving your power to the external world, over which you have no control.

All of that is about to change. We need to work from the inside out, not the outside in.

Why change your food language? Research shows that positive and effective self-talk can:

- improve your self-esteem, stress management and wellbeing

- reduce symptoms of depression and anxiety

- improve your body image

- treat eating disorders, and

- reduce your risk of self-harm and suicide.

Your mind is a garden

It's time to nourish your mind and retrain your brain so you can grow into a beautiful flower, and not a thorny weed. The grass is greener where you water it; your mind is about to become a much greener place, a place you want to be, not somewhere you run away from.

I use the term 'thorny weed' to refer to a person who's constantly putting other people down and projecting their own negative thoughts and feelings outwards on others. If you've experienced this, don't worry. When people are projecting negative emotions on others, it's usually because the other person represents what they aren't and what they want to be.

We all know a thorny weed and we don't want to be one. If you were a thorny weed that has turned into a flower—good on you! I'm super-proud, because I know that change isn't easy.

So, make the promise to yourself now to join my garden of beautiful flowers and nourish your mind with me. If you're a thorny weed or have thorny weed tendencies, pour weed-killer on that part of you and plant fresh seeds for a new garden.

Okay! Now that you've decided to get rid of any thorny weed tendencies, let's do some mental gardening to ensure you have a strong base to grow a beautiful, flourishing garden. Remember: a gardening needs ongoing maintenance, so these strategies have to be applied regularly to work, not just once!

How to change negative self-talk

Remember my slogan 'Awareness precedes change'? Yes, because I've said it a thousand times. To change negative self-talk, improve our food language and build that strong base for our garden, we first need to become aware of how we talk to ourselves. So much of it is subconscious. Start noticing the words you say to yourself, and pick yourself up on it. ('Pick yourself up', not 'beat yourself up'.)

I'm going to give you my top strategy for managing your words when it comes to escaping Food Jail. Notice, I said 'managing' and not 'stopping', as the thoughts may never stop completely. Every day may present a battle and a choice you need to make. However, if you actively manage negative self-talk when it comes up, the frequency, duration and severity of the thoughts will decrease over time.

Here's an acronym I created to help you—AWARE. I developed my AWARE technique from a range of useful psychological interventions, using only the best principles and therapies and refining it over years. The technique incorporates cognitive behavioural therapy, mindfulness and solution-focused therapy to change negative self-talk and improve your food language—thus improving your relationship with yourself and your feelings. It WORKS.

AWARE stands for:

- **A**wareness

- **W**itness

- **A**nother way

- **R**estructure

- **E**ject and execute.

A for awareness

The 'A' stands for 'awareness'—first we want to become AWARE, without judgement. Start to notice the words, sentences and sayings you say to yourself and write them down. Notice:

- Do the same words or thoughts come up often?

- When does each thought come up?

- How do you feel when you say this to yourself?

- What do you do or feel like doing when you speak to yourself this way?

You might, for example, notice you often have the negative food-language thought, 'I can't find a partner because I'm too fat.'

W for witness

The 'W' stands for '(be a) witness' or 'witnesses'. Witness your negative self-talk without judgement or attachment. Rather than being caught up in it, take a step back, almost like you're a jury and your thoughts and feelings are on trial.

Notice each thought from a distance, then ask yourself: Are there any witnesses who could prove in a court of law that this thought or these words you say to yourself are true? Ask yourself what evidence you have for and against the thought. Work through it like this:

Could a witness prove in a court of law that it's true that (to use the earlier example) 'I can't find a partner because I'm too fat'? Let's look at the evidence for this thought:

'I actually have no evidence. A man has never said to me that my weight is a problem, or I'm too fat. It's just me who thinks this. So, no, I can't prove that my weight is the reason I can't find love.'

Now, ask the opposite: are there any witnesses (including yourself) who can prove the opposite of the thought? What's the evidence against this thought?

'I've had relationships in the past and they were very good, despite my weight. Even when I was thinner, my relationships and ability to attract men weren't any different. And I still always thought I was too fat, no matter how thin I was!'

A for another way

The next 'A' in AWARE stands for 'another way'. What's another way to think about this thought? If a friend or family member had this thought, what would you say to them? How would you support them? If your sister said, 'I'm too fat to find a partner', what would you say to her?

Once you've considered this—apply it to yourself. Force yourself to think in another way about your negative self-talk, and use the real evidence you gathered against this thought in the 'witness' section. SAY IT OUT LOUD:

> 'Well, I did go on a date last month and it didn't work out, but it wasn't because of my weight. We just had different ideas of the future. I also do get swiped on dating apps and have good conversations with men, despite my size, which they can see in my pictures. Also, my ex-partners had no issue with my weight—they actually said they loved my curves. It is all in my head, really.'

R for restructure

The 'R' stands for 'restructure'—meaning, it's time to restructure the thought. Remember, you cannot build a beautiful house on a crappy foundation. You need to restructure the foundation of you.

To do this, you need a new and more effective thought. Remember, though—it's not about 'thinking positive', it's about taking what you witnessed above and creating a more wholesome and effective thought. Going back to our example thought, 'I can't find a partner because I'm fat'—let's say this is your thought and you are actually overweight according to your BMI (body max index). This doesn't mean it's the reason you can't (according to the thought) find a partner. The connection you made between body weight and ability to attract a partner is false.

A new, more balanced and effective thought might sound like this:

> *'My weight isn't a reflection of my potential to find a partner. I've had previous partners and my weight wasn't a factor—in fact, they said they loved my curves. I'm putting this pressure on myself, and it's actually demotivating me from even trying to look for a partner!'*

E for eject and execute

The 'E' in AWARE stands for 'eject' and also for 'execute'. You need to eject the old thought out of your mind and execute your new self-talk on a daily, hourly and weekly basis.

Every now and then, old thoughts and beliefs are going to pop up, as they've been the default setting in your brain for a long time. I want you to see them as old TV episodes, movies or songs that you're over. Any time the old tape of your negative thoughts pops into your mind, I want you to imagine your mind as an MP3 player or DVD player (if they still exist—or maybe you're playing a Netflix show called Food Jail at First Sight). When the 'You ate so bad today' or 'You're not good enough' movie or song starts playing in your mental DVD or MP3 player, you need to eject it! Immediately eject the DVD, unsubscribe from the song or hit 'stop' on Netflix.

Next, execute the new thought you created. Repeat it over and over— as many times as it takes to learn the lyrics off by heart. This new, effective thought will become like a Justin Bieber song you can't get out of your head.

But Steph, what if I don't believe the new thought?

You may not believe that getting eight hours of sleep is optimal—but you can still do it, right, and reap the benefits?

You do not have to believe a thought in order for it to be effective.

'Faking it until you make it' is a massive strategy in psychology. In order to make a significant change in your life you may need to fake it until you make it, and that's okay: it's proven to be effective.

Ever winged it through a meeting or job interview, acting like you're confident and the perfect candidate for the role, even though deep down you're like, 'Oh my god, what did they even just ask me?!'? You pulled through and did a pretty good job, right?

Ever made it seem like you had your shit together at a meeting or catch-up, when you were actually hungover and about to die? That's you faking it until you make it—and you made it!

Think about a time in your life when you were successful (in a relationship, job or task) and you felt really good. Take your mind back to this time and visualise it. What can you see, hear and feel? What was your body language like? What were your facial expressions and your behaviour when you felt successful? More importantly, what was your mindset like?

I bet your posture wasn't hunched over with no eye contact. So, when you need to 'fake it till you make it', try to tap into those 'successful' body language and facial expressions.

The truth of the matter is—there's no magic day that you wake up and 'accept yourself'. There is no magic day you wake up 'happy with your body'. There is no magic day you wake up feeling worthy and good enough. You're not going to just wake up one day and start loving yourself and thinking positively about yourself—I'm sorry, it's just not going to happen. I've waited thirty years, and the magic day still hasn't come!

Why wait, though, when you can create? I've created my own magic, and you will too. You have to choose now to fake it; it doesn't matter if you don't believe your new self-talk. Again: you do not have to believe something in order for it to work or be effective.

Repeat, repeat, repeat

Whenever an ineffective thought creeps in, you need to execute the AWARE plan and practice the new thought—over and over again. To retrain your brain, you have to practise daily until it becomes a habit, like brushing your teeth.

So, the next time a negative thought comes up, rather than just jumping on that 'thought train' and going for a negative ride, you're going to choose to step off the platform in your mind and watch the negative thought train go by.

You are not your thoughts, and you can step away from them.

Once you have your new, effective thought, you execute it at every opportunity you can. The more you eject negative thoughts and execute more effective ones, the better you'll rewire your brain. This is 'neuroplasticity' (the ability of the brain to change): the new, effective thoughts will consolidate in your brain and become your new default setting.

Right now, your default setting is likely to be 'negative, defective and ineffective'—and it's likely to have been like that for some time. So, executing the new thought will be tricky to do at first: it'll feel unnatural and maybe a little silly. But... wouldn't you rather feel silly and happy than cool and miserable?

If you think it's unnatural and silly, use the AWARE technique to change this thought, too!

There is no escape from the effectiveness of my strategies. I promise you— it works and you will be so much better and much more likely to engage in life when you practise AWARE. Remember, too, this is not just about food or weight! You can use the AWARE technique to kick any unproductive thought habit.

Using AWARE to destroy black-and-white thinking

Black-and-white thinking is also referred to as 'all or nothing thinking'. In your food vocabulary, it often manifests via the words 'good' and 'bad'. These are two of the most detrimental pieces of food language you can use! You label things at one extreme or the other, with no room for a grey area. Other examples of black-and-white thinking use words like 'never' and 'always'—'You never call me', 'I'm always the one doing the chores'.

Black-and-white thinking in Food Jail (or life in general) insinuates that things fall either into one of two categories: good or bad. This is dangerous, and needs to stop. No-one can be 'good' all the time or 'bad' all the time.

Examples of black-and-white thoughts around Food Jail include, 'I ate so bad on the weekend' or 'I ate so good today'. These have more of an impact on your feelings and behaviour than you might think. When you tell yourself you've eaten 'bad', you subconsciously equate that to 'being bad'—and when you think you're bad, you experience negative feelings like guilt, shame, disgust and disappointment. This can lead down a dark, negative spiral of behaviours that are detrimental to your wellbeing.

And a newsflash:

Food is just food.

We all know that sometimes we're going to eat foods which may not be 'healthy' but which taste good; sometimes our soul needs it. Eating unhealthy foods in moderation is actually mentally healthy and reduces binge-eating behaviour, because there's no restrictive mindset.

Also, think about it: as children, we're given ice cream or lollies to calm us down or distract us from a negative emotion. We learned to associate pain with pleasurable food from a very young age—especially sweets. This association takes time to change, so be kind to yourself. There's nothing wrong with you because you eat a tub of ice cream when you're upset. This is an ingrained psychological habit: your brain has been subconsciously programmed to crave sweet, sugary food when it experiences negative feelings. It's a learned response that has been strengthened over time from repeated pairing.

Life is not about eating clean all the time. I repeat—life is not about eating clean all the time and this will not make you happy, despite what you might think. Allowing yourself to indulge in food and being okay with this, even though it may not feel right or comfortable at first— that's how you stop disordered eating long term.

Applying AWARE

Let's learn now how to apply the AWARE strategy when you get stuck in a black-and-white thinking trap.

1. Awareness

Start to notice when you use the words 'good or bad' in relation to food or any situation, and be quick to pick up on it and write it down. Keep a hard-copy thought log on you or write in the notes section of your phone.

Let's say the black-and-white thought is 'I ate so bad today'.

2. Witness

Step back and witness this thought from a distance, as though it's not your thought, just something you've been asked to observe. Become a witness in a court of law and ask yourself, is there any evidence for this thought? What would other witnesses who saw what you ate that day say about this thought?

Remember, as a witness, you need to examine the evidence for and against the thought. For the example thought, 'I ate so bad today', it might look like this:

- Evidence for the thought:

   'Well, I ate pizza today—but pizza isn't "bad". It might be an unhealthier choice in comparison to a salad, but it's just a food.'

- Evidence against the thought:

   'I didn't drink or have dessert; instead I went home and had fruit, so it wasn't all bad or unhealthy.'

- What witnesses said:

   'My friends actually said it was great to see me let go a little and eat pizza, and that I was looking really happy. They usually see me unhappy with my body and turning down foods I really want to eat.

   'Besides, I don't often have pizza, and I had a really fun night with my friends and woke up feeling good. It was so nice to not rely on how I looked to determine how I should feel. I actually did not binge after I ate the pizza, either, and usually pizza is a trigger food for me. I felt happy and didn't binge—and that's an achievement in itself.'

3. Another way

Now you want to consider another way to think about this thought. Remember that it's not about 'positive thinking': you need to think about this in another way that is realistic, validating and effective.

A more effective way to describe the black-and-white thought 'I ate so bad today' could be:

> *'Well, even though I didn't eat ideally today, that doesn't mean I've eaten bad and I am bad. It's good to have a balance, and I need to focus on the fact I didn't binge, which is a huge accomplishment.'*

This response acknowledges your thoughts and feelings in a much less harsh and judgemental way and helps you focus on what you did well, as opposed to what you could have done instead. How much better does that response sound and feel?

4. Restructure

Next, you restructure that old, ineffective, black-and-white thought of 'I ate so bad today' to something more effective. You'll substitute the new, restructured thought for the old thought in all future self-talk, utilising all the evidence and work you've done in the previous steps.

Your restructured thought might sound like this:

> *'Although pizza isn't the healthiest option, it's okay to enjoy a pizza with my friends on the weekend. This can be healthy in other ways, such as healthy for my soul and social life. Eating pizza doesn't mean 'I ate bad all day', either, because I did have salad and other healthy foods during the day. Even if I did eat unhealthily today, that does not mean it's bad and I'm bad. I'm proud that I have more balance in my life and am being more social with my friends.'*

5. Eject and execute

Finally, you eject the old thought and execute the new thought over and over, and follow it through with an effective behaviour. The minute you hear the 'I ate so bad today' song come up on your mental playlist, you eject it and substitute your new thought. Follow this thought through with an effective behaviour, such as texting a friend, journalling, reading or going for a walk. This behaviour gets you out of the current state and into a productive one that is not eating for reasons other than hunger.

Questions you should frequently ask

There'll be times when you get stuck on a thought or activating event and you're not sure how you feel or think about it—all you know is that you're feeling crappy. That's okay: be kind to yourself if you can't always figure it out.

Sometimes there is no reason as to why we feel a certain way—it could be the time of month, hormones, subconscious factors you can't readily identify or the full moon! Regardless, there are questions you can ask yourself to help you distance and dispute a thought that isn't effective. Keep these questions handy on your phone. The quality of your life is determined by the quality of the questions you ask yourself!

When you're experiencing an unhelpful thought, ask:

- Is this thought helping me or harming me?

- How is this thought making me feel?

- What do I want to feel instead?

- Is this thought effective for me and what I want?

- What can I think instead?

But how do I stop the thoughts?

You might be thinking, 'But how do I stop the thoughts?' As I mentioned earlier, you can't stop the thoughts—and that's not the goal. Trying to block out thoughts, in actual fact, makes them more intrusive. For example, if I told you to think of anything but a black-and-white elephant, all you're going to think about is the elephant! See, I know you're thinking about a black-and-white elephant right now.

Thoughts are like family. You can't choose the ones that come up, but you can choose the ones you spend the most time and effort with. Think about how you feel after you've spent time with someone who's negative. Not good, right? The same thing happens when you spend time with negative, ineffective thoughts. Choose your thoughts wisely!

The goal is to recognise unhelpful thoughts, label them as ineffective and implement a strategy to reduce the distress that they cause.

When you're tempted to block out negative thoughts

If you notice the urge to repress, ignore or block out a negative feeling or thought, I want you to repeat the below mantra.

My goal is not to stop the thoughts. The goal is to ask myself if this thought is effective. If it's not, I will let it go. My thoughts are not facts and I can choose which thoughts I give power to.

My thoughts do not have power unless I give them power.

Your goal is to nourish your brain with thoughts that will help it flourish.

Chapter 25
EMERGENCY RELIEF

Sometimes you need immediate relief or 'space' from your thoughts and need an express technique to deal with negative thoughts. You may not be in a place to apply the full AWARE strategy—maybe you're in a meeting, about to walk in to work, or you're on the phone to someone. For example, say you're in a work meeting and have the thought, 'Don't share your idea, people will think it's stupid'.

Don't worry, I have you covered! I have the ultimate express strategy to save you in less than a minute. Let me introduce you to the big D—the distancing and designating or 'DD' technique. It will give you immediate space and perspective so you can get shit done.

The distancing and designating technique

The distancing part of this technique is putting some metaphorical distance between you and the thought, by inserting 'I am having the thought that...' in front of your thought.

Sounds simple, right? Simple, yet super effective and significant! Try it right now if you don't believe me, and feel the pressure valve release.

For the earlier example of the work meeting and telling yourself not to share your idea, the technique would sound like this:

> *'I am having the thought that I shouldn't share my idea in this work meeting because people will think it's stupid.'*

Immediately, you'll feel like you've taken a load off your shoulders and you will speak up in that meeting. This is the 'designating' part of the technique. Once you've inserted the distance, you must follow through with a designated action—in this case, sharing your idea in the meeting.

The designated action must be done quickly, before your illogical brain can catch up and try to stop you. You have under a minute to access and use the power of the big D!

Practice this as much as you can, until it becomes an automatic process, like brushing your teeth. It will feel weird and uncomfortable at first, but you'll be so glad you did the designated action instead of thinking about it for God knows how long.

You only regret the actions you don't take.

Here's another example of applying the distancing and designating technique. Say you're single, standing in a bar and spot an attractive person you want to approach, but think, 'They'd never go for me.' Insert 'I'm having the thought that' in front of the sentence—so, it becomes, 'I'm having the thought that the person at the bar would never go for me.'

Remember, a thought is not a fact.

Then, you have five seconds to take the designated action—approaching the person at the bar. You have under a minute to harness the power of the big D, so take action quickly!

But what if something bad happens?

You might be thinking, 'But what if I get rejected by the person at the bar?' or 'What if someone shoots down my idea at the meeting?'

First, you have no evidence that this will happen, and if you're going to live your life by 'what ifs', then what if the person at the bar likes you, and you live happily ever after? You can choose which 'what ifs' you give your time and attention to. Choose the effective ones. Second:

Choose your pain.

What's more painful: the temporary pain of getting rejected or the lifelong pain of never trying? You need to choose which pain you want to experience. You won't know unless you try! I would rather die trying than die knowing I never tried at all.

Don't get paralysis by analysis—which is spending so much time justifying and rationalising things to make yourself feel comfortable that you never take action. Remember, temporarily reducing your anxiety by avoidance will increase the anxiety in the long term, and stop you living your full potential! Trust me, you'll regret the times you didn't take action, not the times you did. And each time you take action, your confidence in taking action will grow.

Now that you've learned some methods for managing your conscious thoughts, let's dig a little bit deeper—into your subconscious mind.

Chapter 26

THE SUBCONSCIOUS

Think of your mind as an iceberg: the tip above water is your conscious mind and the rest of the iceberg, below the water, is your subconscious and unconscious mind. There is also the preconscious mind, located just below the conscious, but for the purpose of this book, I will stick to the conscious, subconscious and unconscious.

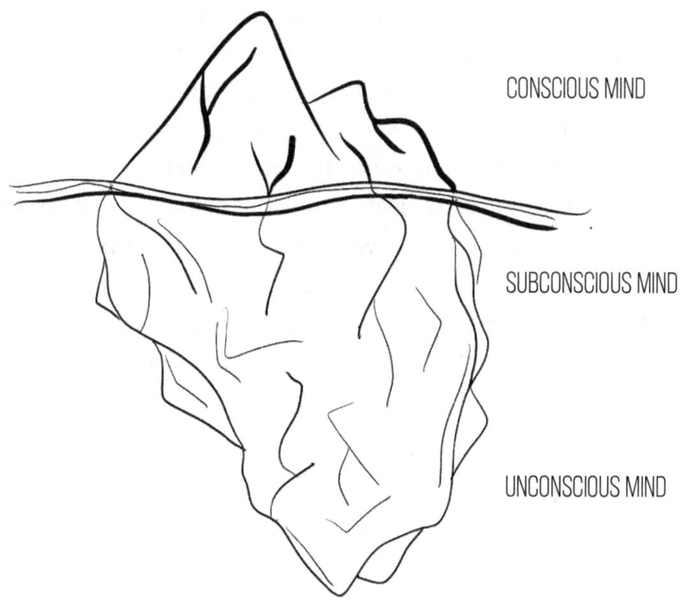

The subconscious mind is a powerful force, driving all our automatic movements and behaviours. Let's take a deeper dive now into Sigmund Freud's three-level model of the mind.

Level 1: the conscious mind

The conscious part of the mind is all the thoughts and actions that you're immediately aware of. For example, you might be admiring the colours and beauty of a sunrise and the smell of the breeze.

Level 2: the subconscious mind

The subconscious is the part of the mind where reactions and automatic actions happen without your immediate awareness, although you can become aware of them if you think about it. For example, do you remember when you learned to swim or ride a bike? When you tried to learn a musical instrument or memorise the lyrics to a song? Usually, the first time you attempt a new set of actions, it's quite difficult. I bet you remember everything about your first experience of learning to ride a bike or swim. I remember my first time trying to ride a bike—it was bumpy, scary but super-fun! I remember my surroundings, the exact park I was in, the track, the trees and my dad pushing me fast, even though I was petrified and felt like I was going to fall off and die!

Once we become more skilled at an activity, it needs less of our conscious awareness, and everything begins to flow naturally. It's like driving a car—remember how aware you were of your surroundings when you were a learner? I bet you remember your first lesson and your driving test like it was yesterday. Now that you're experienced, though, you probably arrive at a destination and don't even remember the drive there, right? This is because you can drive automatically, using your subconscious mind, while your conscious mind thinks about that work meeting you're on the way to. Once you get skilled enough at driving, you stop thinking consciously about which pedal to press, which gear to use or which side the indicator is on. However, you can become aware of what you've done if you think about it.

Another example is wondering whether you left the stove on—most times you can think back and remember whether you turned it off. Though sometimes we still go back home to double-check!

Level 3: the unconscious

The unconscious mind contains all our past memories and events, locked away out of your conscious awareness. These memories and events are inaccessible to you no matter how hard you try to bring them up—for example, the first word you learned to say as a baby or the first time you walked on your own. Your parents might have stories about these things or even videos of them, but you yourself can't access the memory.

Why the subconscious is so important

Your subconscious mind is where most of your negative self-talk happens and is outside of your immediate awareness.

Negative self-talk can increase your stress levels, affect your mental health and even weaken your immune system. It's honestly just not worth thinking negatively about yourself—you have absolutely nothing to gain and a lot to lose! This is why you need to practice my AWARE technique regularly—even when you don't feel like it, which will be often at first.

At times, using AWARE will be harder than at others, and that's why I've included the previous chapter on the distancing and designating technique, and also the next two chapters, which provide additional tools and techniques to assist you in distancing yourself from negative self-talk. You'll learn how to put a shield between yourself and your negative self-talk—it doesn't remove the danger that's lurking, but it protects you.

Remember, your thoughts do not have power unless you give them power.

Like the distancing and designating technique, the following strategies I'll go through are great if you're time-poor and need quick relief from a negative or ineffective thought that has hijacked your mind.

Chapter 27

MINDFULNESS AND THE SUSHI-TRAIN TECHNIQUE

The distancing techniques in this book have been developed based on the most effective psychological frameworks, including mindfulness and meditation.

So, let's talk about mindfulness—a word that's almost overused in 'pop psychology'. However, mindfulness is good stuff and we all need more of it in our day-to-day lives. Mindfulness is the act of paying full attention in a given moment, purposefully and without judgement. It's the practice of noticing thoughts, feelings and sensations without changing them or judging them. It's about knowing where our attention is and being able to choose where we direct that attention. In *Mindfulness for Life*, a book by Dr Stephen McKenzie and Dr Craig Hassed, the authors give a more technical definition of mindfulness as 'attention training' or 'attention regulation'. Just as exercise is crucial for a healthy body, mental training or mindfulness practice is important for a healthy mind and life.

The reason mindfulness is so difficult is that we've been trained to believe that 'multitasking' is effective and if you're not doing three things at once, you're losing time!

What's the difference between mindfulness and meditation?

Mindfulness is simply a form of meditation, and has been around for thousands of years. It has just exploded massively over the past decade due to research on its daily applications and the benefits it provides. Mindfulness and other forms of meditation involve mental training that increases not only our awareness, but also our attention and ability to focus this attention. By regulating our attention, we can avoid being distracted by what makes us unhappy.

Let me repeat that—by regulating our attention, we do not get distracted by what makes us unhappy. Too many people focus their attention on what they don't want—on what makes them unhappy.

The link between mindfulness and the subconscious mind

As I mentioned in the previous chapter, the majority of our negative self-talk is automatic and outside of our immediate awareness. You can be having a great day and then your mind can be hijacked out of nowhere and tell you that you're not good enough. Thanks, mind! This occurs in level 2 of our mind, the subconscious.

By practising mindfulness, you can become more aware of these subconscious habits, and this awareness facilitates change.

How to practise mindfulness

Mindfulness can be practised in a variety of ways—you can literally implement a mindful practice anytime and anywhere. You can eat mindfully, walk mindfully and work mindfully. The aim is to do one thing at a time without distraction and without judgement about what thoughts and feelings come up. It's about noticing, letting go and bringing your attention back to the present moment when the mind drifts off and starts to think of other things—which it always does.

Even if your mind starts thinking about what you 'should' be doing, and you start feeling guilty, you need to notice these thoughts and sensations without judgement and come back to the mindful activity you're doing.

To help you feel more successful in this practice with negative thoughts, I've designed a strategy from my experience with clients that I call the 'sushi-train technique'.

They've reported that this technique is super-effective in any area of life where they have an ineffective thought or their mind is hijacked by negative, subconscious self-talk.

The sushi-train technique

The sushi-train technique was developed by psychotherapist Russ Harris in his book, *The Happiness Trap*: it's a metaphor for unhooking from unhelpful or negative thoughts.

You may have been to a sushi-train restaurant: it's a type of restaurant dining experience where plates of different sushi are placed on a rotating conveyor belt. In the middle of the sushi train is the chef who's creating these dishes and serving them out. As dishes come out on the conveyor belt, you select which ones you like and eat as much as you want. You have your colourful sashimi, your pieces of octopus, your seaweed salad and your traditional tuna or California rolls.

I want you to think of the sushi chef as your mind and the sushi plates as your thoughts, memories and images. Some dishes look appealing and others not so much. For example, think of your everyday thoughts as the tuna rolls, the negative thoughts as the sashimi and your positive thoughts as being the inside-out volcano rolls. These dishes keep coming out, like the thoughts in your mind that come out over the course of the day.

Every day, we are faced with a conveyor belt of thoughts. Like on a sushi train of plates, our thoughts come into the forefront of our mind and awareness. Then like a plate of sushi, they go around the conveyor belt and outside our vision and awareness, then back around again.

Once we've had a look at the dishes, we eventually pick a dish we like off the conveyor belt. Once we pick this dish, our focus and attention centres on it and we experience the dish through our sight, taste and emotion. We eat it, and we either like it or we don't. While we're in this experience with this one dish, all the other dishes become background noise that we don't notice or give our attention to. We're aware that they're still there, going around on the conveyor belt, but we don't let these dishes take our focus away from the plate we're eating.

In the same way, we can choose which 'sushi plates' of thoughts we decide to pick up and engage in. The difference is, when you eat, you're likely to only pick dishes that look appealing: you're able to let the ones that don't look appealing pass by and not give them your attention. The same can be done with your thoughts.

I want you to imagine your thoughts being on a sushi training in front of you, revolving around on a little conveyor belt. There is distance between you and the thoughts as you sit on the chair watching them. You are not your thoughts. They're just thoughts going around on a conveyor belt and you get to pick which ones you want to engage in.

Your thoughts might be, for example:

- 'I'm not going to do well at the interview.'

- 'I don't deserve success.'

- 'Are people looking at me weird?'

- 'I'm not good enough.'

- 'I can't lose weight.'

Just notice these thoughts going around and observe them while keeping your emotional distance. You don't have to engage with them. You are not your thoughts; your thoughts are plates of sushi going into your mind and out of your mind, like clouds floating across the sky. They come and they go.

Would you ingest a plate of sushi you know is going to make you feel sick and bad? No—so don't choose to ingest a thought that you know will make you feel sick and bad. If you choose to jump on a negative plate of thoughts, that plate will be all you can see and think about, and no other plates will get your attention.

Through this exercise, you learn to observe your thoughts without getting carried away by them. By observing your thoughts like plates of sushi going around a conveyor belt, you learn to be mindful of them without judgement, and you realise that you don't have to believe thoughts which are not true, nor useful.

The next time you feel upset, worried, guilty or any strong emotion—think of me and the sushi train. We're sitting together at a sushi-train restaurant and noticing your thoughts go by, without judgement. Just notice the thoughts at a distance. Once they go around the corner, you can't see them, until they come around again; and then they disappear once more.

Which thoughts can you watch go by without engaging in them?

When you're tempted to jump on to a plate and get carried away by a thought that is ineffective, I would remind you that it is just a thought, not a fact, and you can watch it go by and get on with your life. It's not worth it to focus on a thought that will harm you instead of help you.

When you engage in a negative thought, it makes you feel negative emotions, and when you feel negative, you're likely to engage in negative behaviour such as emotional eating or binge-eating.

In the next chapter, we're going to address emotional eating specifically and why negative emotions are linked to emotional eating. Once you understand this connection, you'll have the power to change it.

Chapter 28
EMOTIONAL EATING

Only when we feel, can we heal.

As you have learned, feelings influence behaviour. Every behaviour serves a function or purpose. Whether that behaviour is sex, drugs or bingeing on rocky road ice cream, it serves a function—and that function is usually to allow you to avoid facing strong and uncomfortable emotion or to comfort yourself when you experience that emotion.

We all want to get rid of feelings that feel uncomfortable. In earlier chapters, I spoke about how these avoidant behaviours come about. Growing up as a child, if we hurt ourselves, our parents might have stopped our crying by giving us lollies or ice cream. When we went to the doctor or dentist, we were given a lollipop at the end of treatment to reward us for enduring the discomfort.

We do the exact same behaviour as adults subconsciously—we ease our pain with something that hits the 'sweet spot'. For some people it is food, for others it might be alcohol, sex or drugs. We avoid pain with food, behaviours or substances that we believe bring pleasure. The pleasure distracts us from the pain and gives us a dopamine hit, but it doesn't resolve the pain, and it will come back twofold. Then, we need to double the dose of what we need to numb the pain. Soon, one chocolate isn't enough: this is how bingeing, alcohol and drug use increase in intensity, volume and severity.

From childhood, physical and emotional pain is paired with unhealthy foods or behaviours, and we don't know any better. It's not until we become older and wiser that we realise what we thought was helping us is actually harming us. And it's not until we try to change a behaviour that we realise just how reliant we are on it to take away pain and make us feel good—or even just normal.

How many times have you tried to change a behaviour, such as emotional eating, but it is so goddamn hard? Sometimes, it seems like the pain of not engaging in that behaviour is worse than the original pain. This may be true short term, but it's not a long-term, sustainable option.

Why is change so hard? Because of conditioning. There are two types of conditioning you need to understand: classical and operant conditioning. Let's start with classical conditioning.

Classical conditioning

Classical conditioning is learning through association, and usually begins at a young age. To begin with, there's a natural response. There's a stimulus—something happens or appears, and the person responds naturally. For example, a child might fall over and feel pain (the stimulus) and cry (the response): it happens naturally. Let's say that chocolate bar happens to be present, but at this stage it's what's called a 'neutral stimulus', meaning that the child doesn't respond to it. A neutral stimulus could be an object like the chocolate bar, or a person, or even a place.

So far, we have:

- stimulus—child falling over

- response—child crying

- neutral stimulus—chocolate bar.

In the next stage, the neutral stimulus (the chocolate bar) is associated with the initial stimulus, and at this point, it becomes a 'conditioned stimulus'. For example, the child falling over and crying might lead to their parents giving them a chocolate bar. The child then learns to link crying with obtaining a chocolate bar. This pattern—the child falling over, then crying and subsequently receiving a chocolate bar—needs to happen multiple times in order for them to expect a chocolate bar every time they cry.

Finally, the conditioned stimulus (the chocolate bar) is associated with the first stimulus (falling over and pain) to create a new 'conditioned response'—say, a feeling of comfort. So:

$$\textbf{Pain = Chocolate}$$

$$\textbf{Chocolate = Comfort}$$

Over multiple pairings, this association becomes stronger and harder to break. Soon, just eating the chocolate produces feelings of comfort (emotional rewards). Classical conditioning alone makes it very difficult to stop overeating chocolate when upset.

This problem is intensified by operant conditioning.

Operant conditioning

Operant conditioning is where the behaviour is conditioned to happen whenever there is an urge for the 'reward' (in our example) or an urge to avoid a 'punishment'. Developed by psychologist Burrhus Frederic Skinner, the theory of operant conditioning proposes that behaviour followed by pleasant consequences is likely to be repeated and behaviour followed by unpleasant consequences is less so. The more this association is reinforced, the more the behaviour is likely to be repeated.

In other words, and in relation to emotional eating, just having the urge for the reward (feeling comfort, calmed or loved) will result in emotional eating—because you've learned that you'll achieve this feeling each time you eat. This behaviour is conditioned by associating a need to a behaviour that isn't actually needed—you believe you need to eat in order to feel good, so you eat. Over time, the behaviour becomes automatic and compulsive whenever you desire the reward. This is why, despite knowing all the consequences of this behaviour, such as undesirable weight gain and guilt, you still continue it.

Now that you understand how emotional eating develops, you can start to forgive yourself for it. Be kind to yourself and show self-compassion. Next, it's time to take a deeper dive into what emotional eating is, how it manifests and how you can differentiate between emotional hunger and real hunger.

Emotional eating

Emotional eating is eating for reasons other than hunger. It could be eating because of boredom, stress, procrastination or to fill a void we're feeling or not allowing ourselves to feel. Filling this void with food, alcohol or anything physical may create a false feeling of 'fullness' or feeling temporarily whole.

But what happens when you keep filling a hole with newspaper instead of cement? There are leaks, and it's only a temporary fix, but we don't see the hole. Out of sight is out of mind, right?

Here are some signs that you have fallen victim to emotional eating:

- **Withdrawing from social support during times of need.**

  This was me. I never wanted to 'inconvenience' people with my feelings or show that I was anything but a strong, successful businesswoman and honours student. I was studying to be a psychologist and writing a thesis on body dysmorphic disorder—I believed that I had to have my shit together. Well, appear to have it together. What would people think if they knew I was coming home from a successful day and bingeing on inhuman amounts of food?

- **Not using other strategies that might relieve or manage your stress or sadness.**

  Examples could include journalling, drawing, walking, talking or taking a shower: anything that does not involve eating.

- **Not understanding or being in tune with the difference between physical hunger and emotional hunger.**

  Do you not even know if you feel hungry anymore? Or are you constantly hungry? Or do you just not even know how to eat normally anymore? This is a telltale sign that you may be relying on emotional eating.

- **Using negative self-talk related to binge-eating.**

  Remember how we spoke about the vicious cycle of thoughts leading to feelings which lead to behaviour? Emotional eating reinforces dissatisfaction with yourself and preoccupation with body size, shape and weight, which reinforces emotional eating again in an attempt to deal with it all.

- **Cravings for sugary foods or carbohydrates.**

  Changing cortisol levels in response to stress (i.e. flight or fight response) may lead to cravings, especially for sugar and carbohydrates, as these are quick energy sources to deal with perceived stress.

Now, let's go a step further and look at emotional hunger and how it differs from real hunger.

Emotional hunger vs real hunger

Emotional hunger is related to emotional eating, and has certain clues that you can start to be on the lookout for. Let's look at the difference between emotional hunger and real hunger (see table on page 150), so you can become an expert detective the next time you experience a hunger urge.

This table compares the signs and symptoms of emotional hunger versus real hunger.

Real hunger	Emotional hunger
Real hunger starts in the belly and manifests as a physical sensation.	Emotional hunger starts in your mind and mouth. You might think, 'One taste of that chocolate bar and I'll feel better', for example.
Real hunger progresses slowly over time and has a gradual onset. First your stomach might grumble, and then in another hour it may growl.	Emotional hunger is sharp and sudden. You need to eat now! One minute you're going about your business, the next, you're 'starving'.
Real hunger can be curbed with almost any food. Ask yourself, would I eat an apple right now? If the answer is yes, then you are genuinely hungry. The goal is simply to be fed.	Emotional hunger only has eyes for one food. You want chocolate or chips—and only chocolate or chips.
Real hunger is triggered by the fact that you haven't eaten for four hours or so.	Emotional hunger has a trigger, such as getting a negative email or being criticised. Your first response to a stressful, upsetting or challenging situation is to make your way to the kitchen.

As you can see, challenging situations and negative emotions play such a significant role in how we feel, think and subsequently behave. Let's go on to explore how your brain and body work when you're stressed, in the next chapter.

Chapter 29
THE FLIGHT OR FIGHT RESPONSE

The 'flight or fight response' (or 'fight, flight or freeze response') is a term used to describe the intricate workings of your internal alarm system when your brain perceives danger. The problem is, danger these days appears in everything—an intimidating email, being yelled at, or having a looming deadline for a work or university duty, for example.

Your brain doesn't know the difference between a tiger standing in front of you about to eat you and the fact that you're stressing out because you ate five Mars bars, so it acts in the same way in both cases. When your brain perceives danger—which could be anything from a negative thought or image to an upcoming social interaction—it sends messages to the body to get ready to fight or run away (or freeze). This is how the human brain has worked for millions of years and we can't change it.

These messages that the brain sends when it perceives danger are in the form of neurotransmitters called adrenaline and cortisol—the stress hormones. When you sense stress, adrenaline and cortisol go to various parts of the body to prepare them to take action. This is your brain stepping in to protect you, and it's a sign that your body is working properly.

If the brain had a voice, in the moment of perceived danger, it would be delegating tasks to your body, saying things like, 'Hey heart—I need you to pump blood twice as fast to prepare these muscles to fight the danger or run away from it.' You'd start to feel the physical sensations, such as a pounding heart, that we commonly refer to as 'anxiety'.

While these messages are being sent, other parts of your brain are shutting down to conserve energy—including your frontal lobe, which is responsible for logical reasoning and decision-making. Ever felt so stressed that you couldn't think straight or string a sentence together, and got increasingly frustrated with yourself, causing you to stress even more? This is why. Your brain doesn't have the capacity to think: in flight or fight mode, it flips the off-switch on your logical-thinking brain until you are safe (i.e. calm) again. Then it will turn it back on.

Ever felt like you needed to go to the toilet or do a number two when you felt nervous or stressed? Once again, this is your brain flipping the off-switch on your digestive system, because it needs to direct all its energy to making you fight or run from the stressor. Your brain will shut down your digestive system and expel everything in your body in an attempt to conserve energy to deal with the perceived stressor. If you need to go to the bathroom before a date because you're nervous—this is why!

In other words, whether or not a tiger is standing in front of you posing a real threat, your brain perceives the threat as real and your body and mind will react accordingly.

You might experience a rapid heart rate, dizziness, sweating or shallow breathing—all those anxiety symptoms. This is due to adrenaline and cortisol coursing throughout your body to prepare your muscles for fight or fleeing. This cools the body down by sweating and releases adrenaline by shaking or pounding our heart.

During a flight or fight episode, you might also find yourself craving or 'needing' a sugar or carbohydrate fix. This is your neurotransmitter cortisol demanding quick energy to help you fight the stressor—which, remember, could just be thinking about a work meeting tomorrow or reading an email.

We perceive these symptoms as negative, as they do feel uncomfortable—especially if we don't understand why they're happening or what they mean and try to shut them off!

This is why emotional eating feels outside of your control and is so hard to manage—it's happening not only on a subconscious level but also on a biological one, to ensure your survival. Your body and brain just care about you that much, so let's take a moment to be thankful for having working bodies.

In other words, these symptoms are signs that your body is trying to protect you and are not bad, although they can feel bad if you don't understand them or know how to manage them. Once you learn to identify your stress response and understand it, you can learn to accept the symptoms and manage them effectively.

Remember—awareness precedes change.

PART FOUR
FOOD FREEDOM IN YOUR BEHAVIOUR

In Part Three, we learned how to manage your thoughts and program your mind for success. Now it's time to program your behaviour—what you do—to enhance your success with making a change. In this section of the book, we talk about strategies for reducing binge-eating urges, how to use exposure to overcome fears and how to overcome body image disturbance.

Chapter 30
RIDE THE WAVE

You know how to identify and manage ineffective thoughts now, so it's time to learn the ultimate strategy that combines everything you've learned, and takes it one step further. You'll feel proud and accomplished when you RIDE the wave with me!

The first thing you need to keep in mind is that negative feelings, whether emotional or physical, will always come and go whether you like it or not. You can't stop them; you can only manage them. And the more you try to stop a stress response or ignore it, the worse it'll get. With that said, let's learn how to RIDE the wave and manage the stress response effectively and without food! This will end your disordered eating for good.

––––––––––

The *Free Dictionary* defines 'to ride the wave of something' as:

> *'To enjoy the advantage or benefit of a particularly successful, popular, fortunate, interesting, etc., moment or period of time.'*
>
> (idioms.thefreedictionary.com)

You are going to feel successful when you wake up, using this strategy.

To manage emotional eating or any maladaptive avoidance coping behaviour, 'riding the wave' means you surf your urge to engage in bingeing or emotional-eating behaviour. **RIDE** stands for:

- **R**egular eating

- **I**dentify thoughts and feelings

- **D**eep belly breathing

- **E**xecute the AWARE technique

The strategy is something you must practise every day and make part of your day-to-day routine and functioning. It will significantly reduce binge-eating tendencies and eating-disturbance behaviour.

Regular eating

The first part of the RIDE strategy is regular eating. To minimise binge-eating and restriction, you need to be eating regularly and with no more than four hours between meals. Eating more than four hours apart encourages binge-eating.

I don't care what you eat or how much you eat, but you need to be having three meals a day and two to three snacks. This is the structure I recommend to my clients:

1. Breakfast

2. Snack

3. Lunch

4. Snack

5. Dinner

6. Snack

This reduces restriction, which in turn eliminates bingeing and eating for reasons other than hunger. Note: this is not a meal plan.

If you deviate from this or binge, resume the structure the next day. If you binge at night, I need you to wake up and eat breakfast as normal and the rest of the meals as well.

Identify thoughts and feelings

The second part of the RIDE strategy is to identify the thoughts, feelings and sensations that come up for you during this process. You're on the path to Food Freedom and you have your eating structure in place ('Regular eating'); now, start to observe (without judgement) when stress does creep up on you.

Notice what your map of stress looks like and how your symptoms or urges to engage in unhelpful habits manifest. What triggered your stress or negative emotional state? What is it telling you to do, and how are you feeling? You might notice urges to avoid negative feelings, but try to identify what's wrong and notice it without judgement.

Identify these feelings using the sushi-train technique—observing from a distance, without engaging with the thoughts and feelings.

Remember the thought diary you completed in Chapter 21? I want you to do the exact same thing here. Write down how you're feeling, what you're thinking and what behaviours you're tempted to engage in. Here's an example:

> *'I'm observing that I am feeling really overwhelmed and stressed about this work meeting tomorrow. I feel sick in my stomach and I just want to eat the chocolate cake in the fridge because I think it will make me feel better—but I know it never does.'*

Notice the person said, 'I'm observing'—this creates distance between her and her immediate feelings and urges. When we have distance, we can create change. She observed the fact that she was thinking 'it will make me feel better' and acknowledged that 'it never does'. Acknowledging this creates an awareness of what she wants to do. She is paying attention in the present moment, rather than acting on an urge straight away in an effort to get rid of it!

Even just delaying acting on the urge is a massive step forward. If you normally think about cake and then next minute you're face-deep in a Coles chocolate mud cake, delaying by five or ten minutes is an astronomical improvement.

People recovering from eating disturbance generally don't realise how much a small progression matters. In the eating disorder world, what might seem like a tiny mousehole achievement is actually a major milestone, and should be celebrated as such. Be proud of your accomplishments, even if you think they're small—I can assure you they aren't, and every day they take you further towards achieving the overall big picture and goal.

In the beginning, it'll be challenging to completely abstain from acting on an urge, so I want you to try to delay this, as a starting point.

How to delay an urge

To delay acting on an urge during the 'Identify' part of the RIDE strategy, remember to use the distancing strategy: 'I'm having the thought that…' or, 'I'm observing that I want to get face-deep in a mud cake.' Be sure to use this terminology.

Once you've identified your thoughts and feelings, sit with your discomfort and just notice it, as though you're a curious scientist in a lab studying bodily sensations for the first time. Notice your breathing and be intrigued by it, rather than freaked out by it. It's just your body. It's just you. You're okay. You are safe as long as you're with your body at this moment listening to it without judgement. Be there in this moment for yourself, as you would be for a friend. You haven't died from these uncomfortable feelings, so you can sit with them and learn to be okay with doing this.

Deep belly breathing

This next part of the RIDE technique is a strategy to train you to self-soothe when you're experiencing confronting emotions or bodily sensations.

Once you've identified what is going on for you, without avoiding it or judging it—I want you to take deep breaths into your belly. What's super-important is pushing your stomach out on the inhale, and letting it go down on the exhale. It's the opposite of how you'd normally breathe.

When my clients say, 'I've tried breathing and it doesn't work', I ask them to show me how they breathe—and 95 per cent of the time it's incorrect. No wonder it's not helping!

The incorrect way to breathe

People usually breathe up and down into their oesophagus: this promotes shallow breathing and hyperventilating, which increases anxiety. Did you ever, as a kid, try to breathe through a straw? I have no idea why we did this, but it's exactly what a panic attack feels like! It's incorrect breathing, and the reason people believe that breathing doesn't work.

Your belly as a balloon

You have to breathe out and in to your belly, not up and down into your throat. When you inhale into your belly, I want you to imagine that you're trying to inhale a balloon with your belly. The weird thing is that you must push your belly out on the inhale.

Your belly becomes the balloon, growing big during the inhale. On the exhale, imagine your bellybutton is the balloon opening—you open your bellybutton valve and your belly deflates as you exhale. It doesn't matter whether you breathe through your nose or your mouth—do whatever is comfortable.

Deep belly breathing is also called 'diaphragmatic breathing', as it happens in your diaphragm and not in your chest. Here's is a diagram to show you what it looks like:

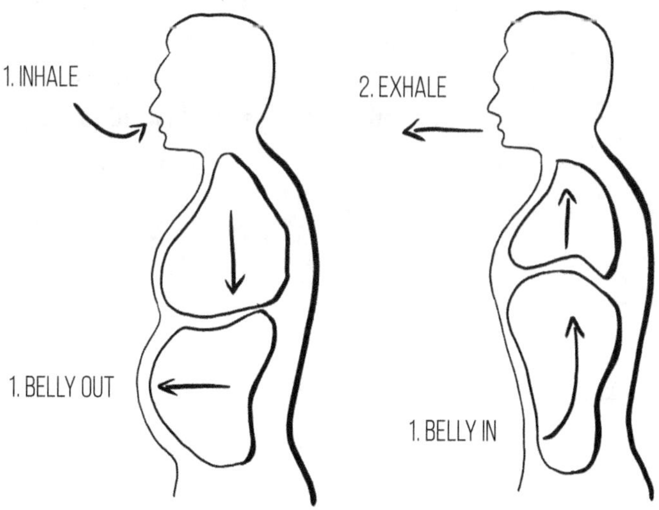

Aim to do at least five to ten deep belly breaths, up to as many as you need to. Try it now.

After you've tried it, ask yourself two things:

1.   How do I feel?

2.   What was I thinking about during that time?

What you'll notice is that you weren't thinking about that work meeting tomorrow (or whatever else was bothering you)—all you were thinking about was pushing your belly out and breathing. Deep belly breathing works to calm you down for two reasons:

1. It takes your mind off whatever's stressing you.

2. It regulates your amygdala.

Biologically, deep belly breathing 'massages' or regulates the amygdala, which is the part of the brain that triggers your flight or fight response when you're thinking about that work meeting. The amygdala is the boss that tells the neurotransmitters adrenaline and cortisol (our stress gatekeepers) that everything's okay and they can stand down. When you do deep belly breathing, you give your amygdala a nice massage so it relaxes!

Psychologically, when you massage the amygdala with breathing and it tells adrenaline and cortisol that you aren't in danger, they open the gate to your frontal lobe, your logical brain. This means you can use your rational brain to manage this situation and use the AWARE strategy from Chapter 24.

Important!

You cannot use the AWARE strategy or any other cognitive (thought changing) strategy if you're in a heightened state, or if your flight or fight system has been activated. You MUST first calm your amygdala by deep belly breathing.

Execute the AWARE tool

The last step of the RIDE technique is to execute the AWARE strategy to work with your thoughts. So, in the example of the person feeling overwhelmed about the work meeting, she would dive deeper into why she is feeling like that—to understand her core beliefs. If she never resolves this, she will continually use binge-eating to manage her stress.

This is why my techniques are so successful—I don't just teach you how to stop the symptom, I work with you to resolve the root cause. It's like treating a recurring rash with topical cream to ease symptoms, but also finding out what is causing the rash and dealing with that. Using RIDE is like the cream—it eases our discomfort while we take the time to address the deeper issues using AWARE.

A quick recap of the **AWARE** strategy:

- **A**wareness of what you're thinking

- **W**itness the evidence for and against the thought

- **A**nother way of thinking about it

- **R**estructure the thought to something more productive

- **E**ject the old thought and execute the new thought and an effective behaviour.

An example

Let's use the AWARE tool for our example woman, who's stressing about her work meeting. Her initial thought was:

> 'I'm observing that I'm feeling really overwhelmed and stressed about this work meeting tomorrow. I feel sick in my stomach and I just want to eat the chocolate cake in the fridge because I think it will make me feel better—but I know it never does.'

Awareness

Why does she feel overwhelmed about this work meeting tomorrow? Let's say she's thinking:

> 'What if my boss thinks my PowerPoint presentation is stupid? This would mean I've failed.'

Witness

We need to find any evidence that this belief is true or, more importantly, false:

- Evidence for the thought—well, there actually isn't any evidence that her boss will think her presentation is stupid.

- Evidence against the thought—her boss has never thought her presentations were stupid in the past. He's actually praised them, and that's why he asked her to do another one.

Another way

Then, we move to asking if there is another way to think about this. We could explore and welcome worst-case scenarios.

Even if, in the worst-case scenario, her boss does think the presentation is stupid, he can tell her in a constructive way that will help her grow and develop. Feedback doesn't mean failure; she can learn and develop from this, if she chooses to.

Another way to think about it is that she's nervous because her work is important to her, and this is a good thing. Feeling nervous could give her the push to get it done!

Restructure

Next, we restructure the thought, using all the information we've gathered, to something more effective and realistic:

> 'I've done well in my presentations in the past. If my boss thinks there's room for improvement, that's a good thing, as I can learn from it. I've done this presentation well before, though, and I can do it again. Being nervous isn't a bad thing: it just means I care.'

Execute

She needs to execute this new thought anytime her overwhelmed thought comes up, and follow through with an effective behaviour such as reading, showering or speaking to a friend—instead of eating a whole cake. She should see if she can delay eating cake at least until she's tried implementing a strategy.

Now you have the cognitive and behavioural tools you need to manage urges to binge, and also to begin understanding your underlying beliefs. Remember, every behaviour serves a function. Once you can understand what that function is, you can work to improve the behaviour or eliminate it as a solution.

You'll have days when RIDE-ing the wave is easy, and other days when it's more difficult. The days you might find more difficult are the days you are 'feeling fat' in Food Jail. If you've ever experienced 'feeling fat', please ensure you read on.

Chapter 31

HOW TO MANAGE 'FEELING FAT'

Now that you've learned strategies to manage urges to eat for reasons other than hunger, as well as how to restructure negative thoughts, let's address another factor that might be keeping you in Food Jail—the 'feeling fat' phenomenon discussed in Chapter 18. 'Feeling fat' maintains dissatisfaction with yourself, encourages dieting and subsequently leads to bingeing and emotional eating.

You might experience 'feeling fat' when:

- waking up after eating a food you didn't want to eat, or thinking that you ate and drank too much the night before

- seeing a photo of yourself in which you 'looked' much bigger than you wanted to

- feeling uncomfortable in your clothes

- a friend has lost weight and you haven't

- scrolling on social media and comparing yourself to others

- you haven't exercised as much as you wanted to and think that you've 'overeaten'.

The first step to manage feeling fat is to change the way you recognise and respond to it. People equate 'feeling fat' with 'being fat', but this assumption couldn't be further from the truth. Here are three steps to stop feeling fat once and forever!

1. Ask what else you're feeling

Feeling fat isn't an emotion, it's a cue to something deeper. So, when you feel fat, it's important to ask yourself what else you're feeling. People fall into the habit of saying they 'feel fat' to describe myriad other feelings without even realising it. It's easy to use it as an umbrella term to describe any undesirable feeling.

Are you feeling tired, sluggish, bloated, hungover or emotionally drained?

Start to track when you're feeling fat—the days, times and the events this occurred around—and try to name what else you were feeling at the time. This is a useful exercise to get you in tune with your mind and body; it also encourages you to extend your vocabulary and understanding of yourself beyond Food Jail.

2. Record the fluctuations

Feeling fat fluctuates from day to day. Record when you experience 'peaks' of feeling fat and ask yourself if anything happened in the previous hour that might explain why you feel this way. Try to identify any triggers, such as being premenstrual, being sleep-deprived or feeling depressed.

3. Tackle triggers directly

When you have done Step 2 and you identified a trigger for feeling fat, you need to target that trigger directly. For example, if the trigger was sleep deprivation, you might have a nap or a rest or speak to a friend. If you target 'feeling fat' instead—which isn't even the real problem— you are likely to engage in restrictive behaviours, which just reinforces dissatisfaction with yourself and encourages dieting, which facilitates bingeing.

When you notice the urge to 'feel fat'—address it quickly and effectively. Remember when I mentioned that your mind will get hijacked by ineffective thoughts or beliefs? This will happen with feeling fat—negative feelings and thoughts will hijack your mind and play the 'feeling fat' movie or song. You need to eject the DVD or song out of your mind by asking yourself what's really going on and then addressing that issue directly and quickly.

An example

Let's say Betty wakes up 'feeling fat' and is tempted to restrict her food intake for the day. Instead, she asks herself what else she's feeling and what happened last night. She finds that she's feeling bloated, tired and hungover from a big night of drinking and eating McDonald's on the way home with her friends.

Betty decides to eject the 'feeling fat' DVD out of her mind by acknowledging that she feels hungover, but this doesn't mean she's fat. She decides to resume normal eating for the day in the form of three meals and three snacks. She shows herself kindness and nurturance and admits that she had a good night and that she doesn't go out drinking often. She takes it easy all day, has a nap to catch up on sleep and feels much better. She's glad she didn't binge and eat her feelings.

Apply these steps whenever you experience the 'feeling fat' phenomenon.

––––––

Now, it's time to target the remaining behaviour that keeps you behind prison bars.

Chapter 32

BREAK THE BARS USING COKE

Food Jail behaviours come in all styles and shapes—I've seen and lived them all. Break these behaviours and you break the bars that keep you in Food Jail.

I know you believe these behaviours are helping you, and you see them as useful, but that's the trick about Food Jail. It's one giant optical illusion that has you under its spell. It's time to ensure that your behaviours don't keep the vicious cycle alive, but instead ensure that it has no oxygen to survive on. The behaviour you choose determines whether you win or lose.

In this chapter, you'll learn how behaviours serve to maintain your dissatisfaction with yourself and encourage dieting and body-checking. You'll also learn how to change these behaviours using my COKE strategy.

Why is Food Jail behaviour so hard to change?

Why is Food Jail behaviour so hard to change? The answer is simple: you've convinced yourself that your behaviour helps you in some way. If you've learned anything up until now, it's how convincing your thoughts and beliefs can be!

Let me give you an example from my own journey.

When I was in Food Jail, I never used to see the value in socialising. I chose to perceive catch-ups and social events as 'detractors' from my ultimate dreams and goals. I'd count down the time until a social event ended and think of all the time was missing out on to be productive. If I broke one of my dietary rules or ate something I believed I shouldn't have at the event, this sent me on a downward spiral, and I'd go home and binge and promise to start fresh the next day.

This is not a way to live, and I changed it. You can too.

Remember the ABCD model? Thoughts lead to feelings which lead to behaviours. So, change begins with having productive thoughts that encourage you down the pathway of Food Freedom. The reason people get stuck for so long is because they think it's their behaviour they need to change—and while behaviours are important to address, this should only be done after you've addressed the thoughts.

Here are common misconceptions people have about what will end their emotional eating and binge-eating:

'If I just stop eating chocolate, this won't happen.'

'If I just stop having "bad" food in my house, this will stop.'

'If I just stop going out with friends, then I won't be tempted to drink and therefore won't go on that Maccas run.'

Notice the word 'just'? I don't like that word and I'm very mindful not to use it, ever. It insinuates that something is easy and we should 'just' do it. If it's that easy—why aren't we doing it? Eliminate the word from your vocabulary now and stop expecting yourself to 'just' do things.

Also, begin to notice if you project this word onto others. I noticed I would always use the word 'just' when I tried to explain to my parents how to use technology—like it was supposed to be easy and they were stupid for not getting it. I realised how horrible this was and stopped! Just because I found something easy didn't mean that my parents did.

Behavioural strategies like not eating chocolate might help short term by creating a false sense of empowerment, but they're a ticking time bomb waiting to explode. When you 'fail', you're back at square one and you internalise this to mean that you're a failure, reinforcing your negative beliefs and thoughts.

It's like taking cold and flu tablets. They make you feel good and believe you can achieve anything, but really they're just masking your symptoms. Once they wear off, you feel groggy and unmotivated and you regret not staying in bed and allowing your body to actually recover.

This is the way the brain and body work and no amount of 'willpower' can fight it. Your problem is not a lack of willpower, so stop thinking you're mentally weak. In actual fact, you're mentally very strong from having to deal with the Food Jail cycle for so long. I know how exhausting and mentally debilitating it is.

What are your remaining Food Jail behaviours?

What behaviours do you engage in that are reinforcing your negative relationship with food and yourself? Following is a list of behaviours you might be engaging in, some without even realising it. Remember, automatic behaviours can develop in our subconscious and occur outside of our immediate awareness. You might not realise that these behaviours are keeping you in Food Jail.

Do you find yourself:

- preferring to eat food you've prepared at home because you know exactly what's in it?

- not going to the movies because you want to avoid eating popcorn or a choc-top and blowing out all your 'healthy' efforts?

- prepping the same food every week because it's 'safe'?

- exercising even when you're exhausted and your body is saying no?

- struggling to take a day off exercising and to be okay with it when you do?

- having a defeatist mindset when you've eaten a food that's demonised as unhealthy and eating it all because you 'stuffed up'?

- eating healthily in public and binge-eating privately?

- eating 'unhealthy foods' in private because you're concerned that people will judge you?

- eating from a pot or pan instead of putting food on a plate, because you think this isn't really eating it or you won't eat as much?

- always going on a diet or planning to turn vegan or keto in an attempt to change your body?

- avoiding events, social situations, birthdays, work drinks or anywhere there'll be food or alcohol so you can try to be 'healthy'?

If you answered yes to any of the above, it's important that you know it may be affecting your life more than you think. Even if you believe these behaviours are helping you, try changing them and see how you feel then. Remember, when you're happy, you're healthy, not the other way around.

You have nothing to lose by trying to do things a different way, and I'm going to teach you how. It won't be easy or feel right at first, of course. Changing any behaviour you perceive is helping you will cause discomfort. This discomfort is often the reason people go back to unhealthy behaviours such as smoking or dieting—because these are familiar and comfortable.

When you have doubts about breaking the bars behaviourally, use this as your mantra:

In order for me to be truly happy, I will experience short-term discomfort. Short-term discomfort means it's working and I'm getting better. Short-term uncertainty and discomfort mean I'm heading in the right direction towards long-lasting progress, happiness with myself and self-worth.

Just like after a gym session, when your muscles get sore and you can't move, discomfort means what you're doing is working. Of course, you put strategies in place to minimise or manage the discomfort—for sore muscles, you eat protein and take salt baths, and in the world of psychology, you do breathing exercises and journalling. Remember, this is a transformation for your mind and you need to look after it. If it feels wrong, it's right.

Let's go on and learn about the strategy that is going to stop ineffective behaviour in its tracks!

The COKE technique

You can change any habit or behaviour (like drinking Coke) using the COKE technique. Here's what each letter of **COKE** stands for:

1.   **C**hoose target behaviour

2.   **O**pposite action

3.   **K**ick unhealthy thoughts

4.   **E**xecute new thoughts and behaviour.

Here's how it works:

1.   Choose the behaviour or habit you're going to change and write down why you're going to change it. This will make you aware of the reasons that this behaviour doesn't serve you anymore. For example:

'I want to stop saying no to social events, because I'm missing out on potential friendships and work connections too.'

2.   Opposite action means that when you're faced with behavioural Food Jail temptation, you do the opposite of what your brain is telling you to do. In our example, the behaviour you want to change is saying no to social events, so rather than declining Friday night drinks, you do the opposite and go—despite it feeling wrong and uncomfortable. For example, you might decide:

'I'll go out with my colleagues after work on Fridays and have one drink.'

3.   Kick unhealthy thoughts to the curb in your mind. They may resurface later, after you've done the opposite action, but for now, make them take a back seat.

Let's say your brain tells you, 'This is wrong. Go back to the old way. If you go out for drinks, you're going to have a bad time! They don't even want you there.' Notice these thoughts, using the sushi-train technique, and then drag them from your mental desktop into the metaphorical trash can in your brain. Imagine your brain as a desktop computer, and you're dragging old documents into the trash. Do this with all unproductive and ineffective thoughts!

4.   Finally, execute your new thoughts and new behaviour—and be your own mental cheerleader, even if you're uncertain or as nervous as hell!

Remember, the human brain is over a million years old and doesn't like uncertainty or change. It's trying to protect you by making you stay in what's familiar and comfortable—but you need to break the bars of Food Jail behaviourally!

The Food Jail mind will try to convince you that this new way of life isn't worth it and it would be much easier to stay as you are. It'll even try to tell you that your new way of life will make you fat, but this is not true. My clients weigh themselves at the start and end of their journey and many stay the same or even lose weight because their body is finally getting some nurturance.

You need to notice these distractions, because they'll always be there, but don't give in or get carried away by them. You can do this using the mindfulness techniques covered earlier (in Chapter 27).

Chapter 33
AVOIDING AVOIDANCE COPING

Avoidance coping, also known as 'avoidant coping' and 'escape coping', is a maladaptive form of coping that involves trying to change behaviour in order to avoid thinking or feeling things that are uncomfortable. Put simply, avoidance coping is trying to avoid stressors rather than dealing with them.

Procrastination is one form of avoidance coping, so if you're a recovering procrastinator or a current procrastination addict, don't worry, I've got you! Procrastination is like a mini-vacation for your brain: it momentarily takes your mind off the stressor and gives you a false sense of relief. Notice I said 'false'. Procrastination is like looking away from a scene in a movie that is scary or undesirable—you feel relieved for a moment—except that with a movie, as soon as the scene is over, you can move on with your life. Over time, however, procrastination (and avoidance coping in general) increases your anxiety, making your list of things to do more overwhelming, which then makes your desire to avoid them even stronger.

You're going to learn to replace avoidance coping with active coping, but before we get to that, let's understand just how ineffective avoidance coping and procrastination is for your progress.

Remember—change happens outside your comfort zone.

The avoidance effect

When you avoid situations that cause you anxiety (such as eating out or socialising, say), your anxiety increases, as does your desire to continue to avoid. This pattern is known as 'the avoidance effect'. So, while avoidance provides short-term relief (and at times can be effective), long term, it creates more significant problems and becomes increasingly difficult to manage.

Avoidance prevents the brain from learning that the feared stimulus or situation isn't an actual threat or dangerous. Avoiding eating certain foods or attending social events, for example, ensures that the fear stimulus is either never encountered or is only encountered for short periods of time before escape is initiated—as illustrated in the graph following. Because prolonged exposure never happens, the association between a non-dangerous stimulus (e.g. eating a new food) and the perception of danger (e.g. weight gain) remains. This obviously keeps the fear response intact and the anxiety and eating disturbance in place.

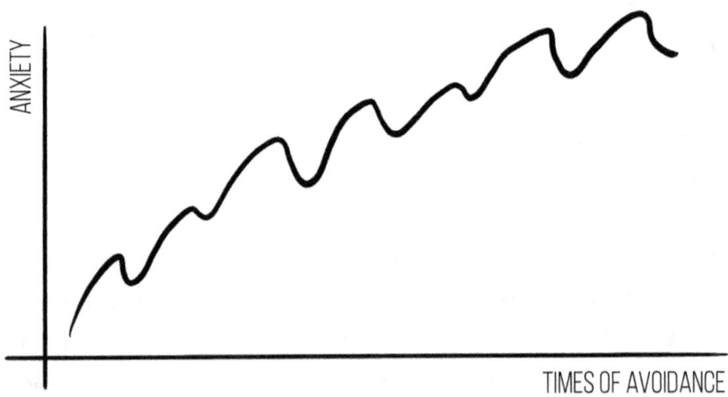

The first step in changing avoidance coping to active coping is—you guessed it—becoming aware of your behaviour. Take some time now to write a list of all the avoidant behaviours you use to make yourself feel safe.

Exposure therapy

Exposure therapy is a psychological treatment that was developed to help people confront their fears, and it's a valuable tool for breaking the pattern of avoidance and fear when it comes to your body and food. Over the next few pages, I'm going to create a safe environment in which to expose yourself to the objects, activities and situations you avoid due to being stuck in Food Jail.

Exposure will reduce your anxiety long term and build your confidence!

Think about the first time you rode a bike without training wheels—I bet it felt super-unsafe and scary, and you might have felt apprehensive about having a second go. With encouragement and praise, you no doubt did, however—and once you practised, riding a bike became enjoyable! You probably wondered how you ever rode with training wheels or felt so fearful of taking them off.

The graph below illustrates the fact that with every exposure task you complete (say, eating a new food or undertaking a new social activity), your anxiety or stress will reduce. During the first few exposures, your stress will be high and it will feel daunting and almost impossible, but I promise it gets easier and easier.

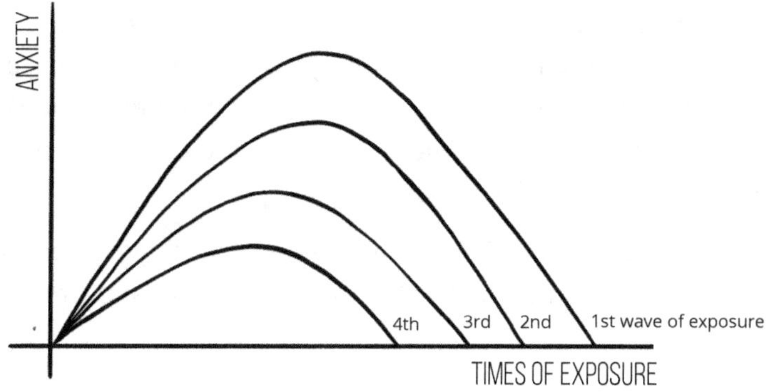

As you can see, during the first exposure, the anxiety reached its highest peak and then it taped off. During the second exposure, there was still an elevated level of anxiety, but not as high as the first time, and once again it declined after the peak. Once you get through the peak, your anxiety will always reduce, especially using the right breathing strategies. Over time, as you get more and more used to the exposure, your anxiety response will decline and you'll feel more and more comfortable.

How to start exposure therapy

Here's how to start with exposure therapy. You'll need the list you wrote earlier of the avoidant behaviours you engage in, so grab that now. Then:

1.   Rate the level of anxiety or distress each of the behaviours on your list make you feel, from 0 (no anxiety) to 10 (extreme anxiety).

2.   Choose the least distressing behaviour and set yourself a small exposure task for this—ordering an entrée at a restaurant, for example. (I help people with this in my Food Freedom course by setting small tasks and working with students to achieve them.)

3.   Reward yourself every time you complete an exposure task.

Take your time when using this exposure technique, as it can be quite intense to do at first. The key is not to feel good or amazing when doing it, though—the key is to do it despite feeling apprehensive. Once the exposure is over, you'll feel good and proud of yourself, and this makes it easier to face it again.

The strategy can be applied to anything you currently avoid, whether it's being assertive in conversations, going on dates or trying a new food group. If you have social anxiety or worry about eating out with friends, for example—make plans with friends, despite your fears, and see them through. You must face the fear.

If you're ever in doubt, do the opposite of what your comfort-seeking brain is telling you to do. If it feels uncomfortable and wrong, you're on the right track!

It's time to find comfort in discomfort and rise above the fears that are controlling your life.

When the temptation to avoid creeps back in

If you're tempted to regress into old habits of avoidance or restriction, remind yourself that this is only temporary anxiety you feel and it will pass. Constantly remind yourself that you're working towards long-term happiness.

Over time, you'll see how much more fulfilling and rewarding your life becomes. Food and anxiety is no longer the life you're accommodating! The goal is to build a life outside of Food Jail.

Now that we've looked at how to deal with avoidance coping, let's address another type of maladaptive behaviour. It's known as body-checking and mirror-checking, and it's something we have all either engaged in or avoided.

Chapter 34

ADDRESSING BODY DISTURBANCE

As we discussed in Part Two, some forms of body-checking and mirror-checking are not useful and encourage dissatisfaction with your body and appearance—which, as you know, encourages dieting.

Mirror-checking is essentially a type of body-checking that, as you'd imagine, involves viewing yourself in a mirror, reflection or shiny surface. Body-checking commonly occurs when you're sitting in a chair, taking a shower or viewing your reflection in a mirror or reflective surface. It could take the form of pinching areas of fat on your body, touching your collarbones or taking comparison photos of your body, or could involve weighing yourself frequently or zooming in on specific parts of your body in the mirror. Body-checking can also involve asking your family and friends about your body ('Have I lost weight?', 'Do you think I look fat?') or comparing your shape to that of others on the street or social media.

Body-checking can feel like a compulsion: something you must do to ensure and reassure yourself that you have not gained weight. It can feel automatic and outside your control and awareness.

You've been programmed to believe that body-checking is useful, but what you need to know is that this is incorrect—it doesn't provide reassurance or relief. In fact, body-checking increases dissatisfaction with yourself, leads to greater feelings of lack of control over your shape and weight, and has been associated with increased anxiety and depressive symptoms. So, any form of body-checking that seems unusual needs to stop right now. Over time, your urges to body-check will diminish.

But I never look at my body!

Body avoidance is just as common as body-checking and mirror-checking, and can be just as detrimental in many ways. Examples of body avoidance include:

- not looking into mirrors

- not shopping for clothes

- not weighing yourself

- not touching your body

- ensuring you don't see yourself naked

- limiting physical contact with other people (e.g. hugging, kissing, having sex).

How to address body–checking and body avoidance

To deal with body-checking, mirror-checking and body avoidance, you need to do two things:

1. Become aware of what you do and how often.

2. Challenge your behaviour.

Let's look at these in more detail.

1. Become a detective

I'm a strong believer in what we measure, we can manage. So the first step to addressing body-checking is to monitor yourself for 24 hours. Pay close attention to how often you engage in body-checking, mirror-checking, avoidance or a combination of these, and write this down. Did you touch your stomach when you woke up, or look at yourself in the mirror? Become aware of your behaviours (many of which you'll find are subconscious) without judgement. Note the time, place and frequency of the behaviours.

Your log of body-checking doesn't have to be perfect: it just needs to promote awareness. Here's an example 24-hour log for body- and mirror-checking.

Time	Type of body- or mirror-checking	Thoughts and feelings
7 am Wake up	Pinch my stomach. Weigh myself.	'I am so bloated.' 'I've gained 700 grams.'
8 am Home streaming workout	View my stomach on the Zoom video.	'I hope the trainers don't think my stomach looks grotesque.'
10 am Shower	Sucking in my stomach in the mirror and pressing it down with my hands.	'I just want my stomach to go down.'
11 am Getting dressed	Looking in the full-length mirror.	'I hope my stomach doesn't look fat.'
Glancing at my reflection in mirror	6 times during the day.	Looking mainly at stomach and arms.
7 pm Bedtime shower	Touching my cellulite in the shower.	'How can anyone ever love me with these bumps on my butt!'

Here's an example log of someone monitoring their body avoidance over a 24-hour period.

Time of day	Type of body avoidance	Thoughts and feelings
7 am Wake up	Partner wants to cuddle and I avoid him by going to the bathroom and getting up.	'I hate when he touches my stomach, it's so disgusting.'
8 am Home streaming workout	Keep my video off so I don't need to see myself working out.	'Out of sight is out of mind.'
10 am Shower	Do not look in the mirror.	'I hate washing my body.'
Getting dressed	Wearing oversized clothes.	'This is comfortable and I don't have to face my body.'
Avoiding any mirrors	5 times a day.	
3 pm	Buying clothes online.	'At least I don't have to try them on.'

2. Challenge the body-checking or body avoidance

Once you know when and how you engage in body-checking or body avoidance, you need to challenge the behaviour by actively asking yourself questions when you're in the moment. The next time you engage in body-checking, ask yourself:

- What am I hoping to find out by doing this behaviour?

- Is it helpful?

- Has anything changed since the last time I body-checked?

These questions will be difficult to answer at first, as you won't always have a logical answer. However, repeatedly asking these questions and challenging your behaviour will decrease the frequency of your body-checking over time.

Strategies to reduce body-checking behaviour

Next, in order to reduce your preoccupation with thoughts about your body shape and weight, you need to begin to reduce your checking behaviours.

- **Gradually reduce the duration** of time spent on the behaviour. For example, if you spend three minutes touching your hip bones, reduce this to one minute.

- **Delay your behaviour.** If you get an urge to body-check, delay this urge by five minutes, then ten minutes, and keep pushing the time out.

- **Limit your checking behaviour.** For example, instead of weighing yourself daily, limit yourself to weighing weekly.

- **Delete the checking behaviour altogether.** For example, stop pinching your stomach in the morning—instead, rub your hands together when you are tempted.

Many of my clients find removing the scales or giving them to a friend or family member helpful. Also, moving mirrors in order to break these habits can be very helpful.

Following is a table to help you reduce body- and mirror-checking. Choose three behaviours you wish to change and write them in the table; then, each day, record the number of times you actually checked. Observe how the numbers go down as the week progresses.

Checking behaviour	Mon	Tue	Wed	Thu	Fri	Sat	Sun
Pinching stomach daily	*Once*	*NONE*	*Once*	*NONE*	*NONE*	*NONE*	*Once*

Addressing body avoidance using exposure

If you're an avoider, it's time to engage in some healthy body exposure. Choose three avoidant behaviours that you want to change—maybe wearing different clothing that shows your figure, looking at yourself in the mirror or having sex with the lights on? Then, for each of these behaviours, rate how distressed you would feel engaging in this behaviour, on a scale of 1 to 10 (with 10 being the most distressed you could feel).

Start working with the behaviour that has the lowest distress rating; as you get better at the body exposure, you can start working on the more distressing ones. Here's a sample table that you can use to track body exposure.

Avoidance behaviour	Distress rating	1st exposure	2nd exposure	3rd exposure	4th exposure
Letting partner cuddle me.	8 / 10	Cuddled for 2 minutes, anxiety 9/10.	Cuddled for 4 minutes, anxiety 7/10.	Cuddled for 5 minutes, anxiety 6/10.	Cuddled for 10 minutes, anxiety 4/10.

It's very important that you start to put yourself in these uncomfortable situations and carry out the behaviour. Change happens outside our comfort zone! Continual exposure will decrease your discomfort and anxiety over time until the behaviour is no longer distressing. Be sure to rate your discomfort and feelings with each exposure, so you can observe the changes over time.

This practice will enable you to build your confidence in any area of your life!

A healthy balance

As mentioned earlier, both frequent checking and avoiding can be an issue. The goal is not to completely avoid facing your body, as this can become equally as detrimental to your wellbeing, because it can negatively influence your self-evaluation. You want to create a balance between checking and not checking.

Examples of healthy body-checking and mirror-checking include:

- using your mirror for a quick overview when you're getting dressed because you want to make sure the clothes fit you appropriately

- weighing yourself once per week (or even less)

- using a face mirror to apply make-up.

Weighing yourself once a week or less can provide a middle ground between over-weighing and avoiding weighing yourself completely. Weighing yourself more frequently can increase dangerous preoccupation, as your weight can fluctuate on a daily basis depending on several factors, including levels of hydration, bloating, constipation, and so on.

Food Freedom

Now that you've learned how to break the bars behaviourally, there's nothing stopping you moving forward and creating a life outside of body shape, weight and food. It's time to push yourself outside your comfort zone and experience long-term progress and happiness! It's time to break out of this cycle and out of Food Jail forever and join me in the journey we call Food Freedom!

Chapter 35

THE TEMPTATION TO RETURN

I know you're motivated to change, or you wouldn't be reading this book, but let's talk about when you're sitting at home alone on a Friday night and you start to feel urges to go back to Food Jail. Maybe you had a bad day or your partner broke up with you; maybe you had an amazing day and want to celebrate! Maybe you ate too much and are feeling like you want to purge, restrict the next day and go on a diet or exercise excessively. This is going to happen—it's normal and okay!

Remember, the key isn't to never experience urges, the key is to manage them more effectively when they do happen.

The thing with eating disorders and disturbance is that they like to try to stick around while you're trying to thrive. As I've said before, you cannot stop the thoughts—the key is to notice the urges and not to be influenced or distressed by them.

I'm not saying that you're never going to binge again, for example (if bingeing is your issue), and in fact, having a binge every now and then is healthy. What is going to change is how you relate to and interpret a binge. You'll continue your life despite the binge, and you won't engage in restrictive behaviour or a guilt trip afterwards. The emotional distress that would come from bingeing or emotional eating will change, and so will the severity and frequency of the binge-eating behaviour.

You're going to experience temptations to go back to Food Jail, because your brain over the years has been conditioned to believe things that aren't true. Whatever your underlying negative beliefs might be—say, 'I need to lose weight to attract a partner'—remember that there's no evidence for this, and that you need to challenge those negative thoughts rather than accept them.

When you feel tempted to engage in a Food Jail thought, action or behaviour, ask yourself these questions:

- Have I tried this behaviour before? Did it work?

- How did the behaviour make me feel?

- Was it sustainable or maintainable?

- Did I lose weight or get my dream body by doing this?

- How do I feel when I'm not doing this behaviour?

This will remind you that your old belief about what you need to do to be happy is actually faulty. Eject that old DVD and do what you know is right.

Every day, hour and minute is within your power and control, and you can choose how you respond to what comes up for you. Respond, don't react. Become your best self: escape Food Jail once and for all and enter Food Freedom with me.

WHO AM I NOW?

After five years of running my fitness business, writing a thesis as part of an honours degree, getting rejected from both an honours and master's degree and dealing with an eating disorder—I became a psychologist. I did it.

I've realised that even now, I don't give myself enough credit for the things I've achieved in my life. I bet you don't either! We are so fixated on moving forward and focusing on the next best thing that we don't stop and say a fucking 'Well done' to ourselves! If we can't stop and reward ourselves for what we accomplish, what are we even doing it all for? I never realised that selling my business for six figures was a pretty damn good achievement. I also mentored, inspired and coached so many women around me.

How did I overcome my eating disorder?

I overcame my eating disorder by embracing who I really wanted to be. I embraced what I loved and missed so much, too—food. I admitted that it was okay to like foods that weren't chicken and broccoli and admit how good they tasted. I slowly ate out more and gave myself a break from wanting to be shredded and lean.

The more I focused on being lean, the most I lost sight of how I actually looked. When I look at photos of myself from this time in my life, I see a fit, healthy girl—but I couldn't see this back then, because my mind was focused on the 'future version' of me that I wanted to be. Why did I need to be skinnier, fitter, better or more desirable? I didn't. No-one was telling me I needed to be a certain way, except me. What was I gaining from this? Dissatisfaction and the feeling of failure.

I discovered that I could be happy just as I was, and maintain a healthy life that was not restrictive or obsessive. Little did I know that doing this would actually change my body.

People knew how much I loved to go out for brunch and asked me all the time where they should go to eat. My passion for food led to me starting an Instagram page in around 2015 (after I became a psychologist) where I would post photos of the best cafes I discovered, so other people could go too. I stopped trying to fight my passion and embraced it. This was also a way I could feel good about what I ate instead of feeling guilty, as people would react to the photos positively. I soon became a go-to foodie expert and brunch queen!

My Instagram page grew exponentially and people wanted to know more about my life. So, I started uploading stories of what I was doing during the day, such as going to the gym or to events. This may seem weird, but it felt so natural and fun for me. Soon I was getting hundreds of views on my stories. People started responding, interacting and telling me they loved to follow me and I inspired them. It was amazing, and encouraged me to keep going. I always knew I wanted to motivate, inspire and help people on a mass scale, rather than one on one in a counselling room, and here I was doing it online without even realising it.

I had my first foodie meet-up in September 2018 with a few other Instagram food bloggers. It was like a first date with the people I met online! This was the day my life changed forever. I met people who genuinely loved food as much as I did and weren't fixated on their appearance, shape or weight. They were actually normal—and they thought I was normal too!

We didn't talk about dieting, the gym or our bodies. We spoke about the latest cafe and dish we ate, and there was no judgement or guilt. Was this the real world, I wondered? All I'd known were the people around me, who were constantly trying to lose weight and diet.

We began to hang out and go to 'food collaborations' together. As my Instagram grew, cafes started inviting me to come and eat! How could I say no? We'd order a range of dishes and for the first time in years, I ate foods that I'd previously deprived myself of—Nutella pancakes, waffles, fried chicken and bread. I was so scared at first, but I forced myself to 'act normal' because I wanted to become normal and appear normal to my new food friends. I acted like the person I wanted to become.

Remember earlier when I spoke about 'fake it until you make it'? The key of life is to act like the person you want to become. It's not, 'What do I need to do?' to overcome an eating disorder, it's, 'Who do I need to become?' and 'I now choose to become this person.' A person without an eating disorder would go out and eat—so I did that. A person without an eating disorder would order what they really wanted—not the healthy dish they felt compelled to order. I took all these steps, despite it feeling super-uncomfortable and unnatural to me.

Apply this to any area of your life and go for it.

Find who it is you want to be—and be that person now.

Want to be a guy with more confidence? Do what that guy would do—ask the girl on a date even if she may reject you. Want to be the girl who's no longer orthorexic? Order a burger with your friends and don't look back! When we continually read the previous chapters of our life, we can't move forward with the new ones.

As time went on, I did more food collaborations and ate different foods and a lot of them—but I actually lost weight and got into the best shape of my life, because I was no longer obsessing over it and my body finally had energy to live. When I was happy, healthiness came as a bonus.

I'd never felt so vibrant and alive and excited, and because I knew that on the weekend I was going to have Nutella pancakes, I naturally made healthier food choices during the week. There was no pressure or resentment to eat a certain way, and it felt so liberating. Finally, I'd been set free from the confines of my prison. I entered Food Freedom, and you can too.

Please note—I'm not saying fried chicken will make you lose weight. I'm saying that when you give yourself free rein to eat what you want, you won't feel deprived and constantly crave the things you don't allow yourself to have. When you eat something indulgent, you won't obsess over it and overdo it. You aren't restricting, and therefore bingeing becomes obsolete.

I would like to also mention, though, that eating out does not 'make you fat'. For years I had personal trainers tell me how bad it was to eat out. I now eat out up to five times a week and 80 per cent of the time I choose healthy options—not because I feel compelled to, but because I enjoy healthy foods and how they make me feel. On some days, I eat Nutella waffles—which are bloody delicious—because they're what my soul needs. As you can tell, I really like Nutella pancakes.

What your soul needs will differ on different days, and that's okay. Feeding your soul means listening to what you need emotionally—so listen to that voice. When I feed my soul with something like Nutella, I savour every bite and feel gratitude in every mouthful. I feel so happy when I eat these foods, because I'm eating out of choice and desire and not out of guilt and resentment. I take my time to eat them and embrace them, instead of rushing so I can pretend it never happened.

My journey to Food Freedom has changed my life, and now I want it to change yours.

Allowing myself to eat what I want, when I want means that I never feel restricted and hence don't have many urges to binge-eat. When I do have urges, I welcome them and choose to notice them with curiosity and kindness. I thank my body for alerting me to something that it needs. I no longer see urges or cravings as an indication that I'm faulty or a failure. If I want chocolate—I have it and enjoy it!

I giggle every now and then when I have a binge, because I'm like, 'damn that was good and I needed it', but I wake up and get on with my life, and you can too! Everyone gets cravings and indulges—even the Insta-fit girls with six-pack abs—trust me, I know them! Remember, it's restriction that leads to bingeing. The more you restrict yourself, the more likely you are to binge.

Because I don't feel stressed about my body or food, my cortisol levels are stable. Cortisol is the double-edged hormone that's activated when your brain perceives danger and activates the flight-and-fight response. When you have cortisol surging through your system all the time, chronically, it can increase your appetite and cause cravings for sweet, high-fat and salty foods, leading to weight gain and a struggle to lose body fat, especially around the midsection. With stable cortisol, I look and feel better than I did when I was obsessed with what I ate and how much I exercised!

When you give yourself food flexibility, you enter Food Freedom and you naturally want to pursue healthy options. When you're happy, you're healthy, not the other way around.

I've put on weight, and I am not upset. I'm grateful, active and healthy. My weight does not dictate my mood, because I choose how I want to feel. You can't build a healthy body from a toxic mind. Trust me, I tried; and now it's time for you to try something different.

It's time for you to enter Food Freedom.

WHERE TO FROM HERE?

This brings us to the end of my first book, *Food Jail*—it's certainly not my last. Thank you for investing your time in it: I truly hope it's been a useful and enjoyable read for you. I look forward to continuing to connect with you and wish you all the best on your journey.

If you enjoyed this book, it would mean the world to me if you could let me know by writing a review.

The Food Freedom program

My Food Freedom course is where this journey continues. It's a supportive online program I developed, offering only the best tools and techniques to help you overcome binge-eating, dieting and having a negative relationship with your body. This program helps you realise how Food Jail works in your brain and how you can escape.

The Food Freedom program is the best thing since sliced bread—really! It will transform your mind and confidence, and help you live your best life and reach your ultimate goals.

I have a special offer on the program to anyone reading this: send me an email at foodfreedom@mindfoodsteph.com with the subject 'Food Freedom' to find out more.

Food Freedom program discount

I'm offering readers of this book a special discount on the
Food Freedom program.
Email: foodfreedom@mindfoodsteph.com

Let's connect!

It's so important to surround yourself with like-minded people in life, and
it's never too late to find your tribe. I'm here to help facilitate that. I know
you want to be part of something great, so I developed the 'Mind Food
family' on my social media.

Website:	www.mindfoodsteph.com
Facebook:	www.facebook.com/mindfoodsteph
Instagram:	instagram.com/mindfoodsteph
YouTube:	https://www.youtube.com/channel/ UCZ5uIXkbnhmJrjW5v_rGOOg
Email:	foodfreedom@mindfoodsteph.com

REFERENCES

American Psychiatric Association, *Diagnostic and Statistical Manual of Mental Disorders*, 5th edn, Washington, DC, 2013.

Arcelus, Jon, Alex J. Mitchell, Jackie Wales and Soren Nielsen, 'Mortality Rates in Patients With Anorexia Nervosa and Other Eating Disorders: A Meta-analysis of 36 Studies', *Archives of General Psychiatry*, 2011, vol. 68, no. 7, pp. 724–731, DOI: 10.1001/archgenpsychiatry.2011.74.

Harris, Russ, *The Happiness Trap*, Exisle Publishing Limited, Wollombi, New South Wales, 2007.

McKenzie, Dr Stephen and Dr Craig Hassed, *Mindfulness for Life*, Exisle Publishing Limited, Wollombi, New South Wales, 2012.

'Other Specified Feeding and Eating Disorders (OSFED)', *Eating Disorders Review*, www.eatingdisordersreview.com/eating-disorders/specified-feeding-eating-disorders.

SUPPORT RESOURCES

Beyond Blue
beyondblue.org.au
1300 224 636

The Butterfly Foundation
butterfly.org.au
1800 334 673

Eating Disorders Victoria
eatingdisorders.org.au
1300 550 236

Lifeline
www.lifeline.org.au
24-hour crisis support line: 13 11 14

Books

Brain Over Binge – also available as an audiobook
Kathryn Hansen

The Happiness Trap
Dr Russ Harris

Mastering Your Mean Girl
Melissa Ambrosini

Overcoming Binge Eating
Dr Christopher G. Fairburn

Self-Compassion Step-by-Step – also available as an audiobook
Kristin Neff

You Are Enough – also available as an audiobook
Mandy Hale